23
. . . and
Finally
Loving Me

----- ❧❧❦❧ -----

by

Tiara Riley

ISBN-13: 978-0-692-98935-7

23 . . . And Finally Loving Me

This is a work of fiction. Names, characters, places, and incidents either are the products of the author's imagination or are used fictitiously. Any resemblance to actual persons, living or dead, businesses, companies, events, or locales is entirely coincidental.

For permission requests, please contact the author via the "Contact" page on the following website: www.nicolesnetwork.net.

Dedication

This book is dedicated to every 20-something who is trying to just figure life out! This is for anyone who has ever felt like they've lost the instruction manual to life and is wondering, "where do we go from here". This book is for you! I just want you to know that you're not alone and please understand it'll get better in the end! I pray you find peace as you begin your journey to discovering genuine self-love and continued self-development!

If you've ever dealt with issues of depression, suicidal thoughts/attempts, overwhelming stress and anxiety, daddy issues, family drama, low self-esteem, and adjusting to life's changes...then this book is for you! As you read through my testimony, I challenge you to reflect on your own circumstances and seek out areas of improvement. Commit to your journey and always look for ways to improve yourself! Ultimately, "Whatever's good for your soul...do that"!

Acknowledgements

God – Thank you for giving me the wisdom to grow and develop into the woman you've called me to be! You've kept your promise to never leave nor forsake me, and for that I'll be forever grateful. I dedicate my life to serving your people!

Mommy (aka Tina) – You have been my rock my entire life, and I love you to the moon and back! Thank you for always pushing me to be the best version of myself and for loving me unconditionally. I appreciate you putting up with all my mood swings over the past couple of decades! Love you!

Talen – To my baby sister, I am absolutely your biggest fan! You continue to amaze me in all that you accomplish in this life! What I'm proud of most is your loving and caring heart and your true aspirations in life! It is my greatest motivation in life to be the best example of #BlackGirlMagic for you to look up to. I hope I'm doing okay! I love you with all of my heart!

To my Family – Thank you for the lessons you've taught me, most importantly for teaching me how to live, laugh, and love. The roads may not have always been easy, but I've learned you stick by family no matter what!

To my Mentors – To anyone who has ever poured into me, guided me, and held me accountable, I thank you from deep in my heart! I firmly believe accountability partners are the key to growth and development; thank you for being that for me in my life. My growth is in large part contributed to being held accountable. Thanks for checking in and asking the hard questions.

My Beloved Sorority – Thank you for teaching me to be the best version of myself and giving me the freedom to grow fearlessly. You've connected me with some of the best women in the world, and through those connections I've gained true sisters along the way. Thank you for never asking me to be someone else, but instead encouraging me to better myself every step of the way. To thee only, Sigma Gamma Rho!

Tiara Nicole– I am so proud of the growth you've experienced throughout life and the person you have become. You are a beautiful person inside and out, and I'm beyond thankful for our journey. You have been stronger than you could've ever imagined, and I hope to continue to make you proud. Your past has created a foundation for my current and our future. This journey to discovering self-love is a lifelong journey and that's what makes it so beautiful! Keep shining baby girl!

Foreword

When I think of the ideal *role model,* I do not think about the person with the most money, cars, or clothes. Instead, I envision a person that has been through trials in life yet has found a way to be an overcomer through fearless determination. In order to be a role model of that nature, one must be willing to share her story amidst possible criticism and judgment. For a role model like this is not afraid to go through the fire just to reach those that need to know her story - and be guided by it.

I am immensely honored and overjoyed that my lifetime Soror and eternal friend, Tiara Nicole, has chosen to courageously make her life transparent to help others realize that life happens, but it is up to you to write your own story. That is exactly what she did.

In this book, Tiara's details what it was like being at a weird age in her life. You know what I'm referring to - that time in your life when you are at a crossroad between self-discovery and self-doubt:

I feel like a failure. All of my friends are excelling, but I am still stuck.

I just do not feel like I am good enough to receive that blessing.

I am there for everyone, but where is everyone when I need them here for me?

For Tiara, that weird age was 23. Though this phase in life may happen to you earlier or later in life, the fact remains that it happens to the best of us. Even as a successful Training and Development Coordinator, thriving blogger, and mother of the best son in the world, I have encountered my own phase like this. Good thing this book isn't titled, "23 and That's All". It will leave you feeling inspired! Flip the page and find out how Tiara learned to love herself at 23 and how you can learn to love yourself through your tough time too!

Tiara dear, you are one of my role models.

With Love and Light,
Tal'Meisha S. Frontis
Founder of the SimplyMei Blogging Site
Member of Sigma Gamma Rho
Founder of the D.I.V.A.S. Organization (UNCC)
Standing Training and Development Coordinator

Author's Note

This book chronicles my 23rd year of life. It begins on my birthday, October 11th, and follows my journey throughout the entire year leading up to my 24th birthday. Each chapter focuses on a different aspect of my growth, and there are sections in each chapter. The paragraphs in each section are not dated, but they are in chronological order to show my growth as the time passes. It's my hope that my journey through this book shows the growth, self-awareness, and self-love that can be achieved through journaling and self-reflection.

Table of Contents

Introduction

My Jordan Year

23. What an odd birthday. It's stuck between 21 and 25 with no iconic meaning. As for me, I intend for it to be the happiest year of my life to date. I'm going make this happen by making a conscious effort to put my happiness first, learn to love myself, and experience everything my heart desires. It wasn't until recently that I realized I didn't love myself, but what's worse is I didn't even know it and certainly did not know how to love myself. I'd hate being alone because subconsciously it made me feel unwanted. I'd choose majors, schools, and even jobs that were just okay because I didn't feel good enough to get what I deserved. I'd behave promiscuously because I didn't feel like I'd be able to get real attention and experience true love.

This year that all stops! I'm going to learn to love myself and learn the true value of my mind, heart, and body. I'm learning that it is honestly better to be alone than to be treated like less than I deserve. It's ironic because I could cut off family members for treating me like crap, but I couldn't see that in the lame guys I'd invite to my bed. This year I plan to question everything and resolve the deep-rooted issues that have caused this disconnect.

The beautiful part of being 23 is the freedom that comes with it! I can quite literally do anything my heart desires without the need to get clearance from, report to, or factor in anyone else in my decision. Although it sounds selfish, this is the time in life where it's okay to be selfish, because my decisions do not impact anyone else in my life, at least not directly.

As I reflect on the significance of this year in my life, I can't imagine how it's become such an overlooked year! People celebrate 21 and 25, but what happens to all the other years in between? How do you develop from the party animal most people are at 21 to the mature adult ready for responsibility at 25? The years in between are critical, otherwise you become the creepy old person drunk at the club, and no one wants to be that person.

As this year is approaching, I feel a constant push for me to grow and develop as a person. Personally, I don't believe in New Year's resolutions, because it's completely illogical! If you have to wait until January 1st to make self-improvements, they're not likely to last. It's such a peaceful feeling knowing that I can work on being a better me anytime of the year. I am very excited to see what this year has to offer me. I feel that I will begin to live the life I've been waiting for and working towards. I'm finally at a place where I can see the seeds I've planted begin to bud.

I Got Goals . . .

There is so much I want to experience over the next year with traveling being at the top of the list! Almost two years ago my family and I went to get passports and mine has yet to be stamped. This MUST change! In addition to the international travel I plan on doing for my birthday next year, I want to do more domestic traveling as well. Although it would be nice to have a travel buddy, I'm willing to go alone.

Speaking of having a travel buddy, friendships are an area I've continuously struggled with throughout my entire life. It's a sick cycle involving extremely high expectations, pushing people away, and an issue with me being overemotional at times. That's something I plan on working on!

I've learned that my home should be my sanctuary of peace and serenity. Gaining that understanding requires me to protect that peace by limiting whom I invite to my house. I used to feel so desperate for company, especially in a 2-bedroom apartment by myself, that anyone willing to visit was welcomed. Now, I have learned the hard way that not all company is good. Before allowing someone to come over, I factor in if his or her vibes will ruin or enhance my peaceful domain. Not only within my physical home, but I'm learning to apply that to my mental, emotional, and spiritual homes as well! It won't be as easy of a lesson to apply, but man it'll be worth it!

Financially, professionally, spiritually, physically, and emotionally . . . I can see things improving in my life and for that I'm thankful. It will be nice to see the fruits of my labor because I have grown and developed a lot. I've come to the conclusion that I probably won't get married anytime soon. I refuse to get married if there is any possibility that I will be unhappy, unsatisfied, or likely to cheat. It's a complete waste of time, and I am no longer that desperate to get married. So, until I meet someone who naturally removes all doubt for me, marriage is not even an option.

Let Freedom Ring

I find myself enjoying freedom so much that I end up craving and fighting for that freedom. I've come to accept that my peace, happiness, and freedom are my top priorities and deserve my utmost protection. Growing up, I never realized the importance of having the freedom of choice and how it impacted my happiness. Nor did I fully understand that my happiness was solely my responsibility, but when you know better you do better! ***Warning*** There is a fine balance between a complete and utter disregard for those close to you and choosing to put yourself first!

I strongly believe that in order to live a successful life it's critical to be self-aware! Personally, it is very rare that someone can tell me something about myself that I'm not already aware of. The key issue for me has been knowing how to use that awareness to grow and develop into a better me. That is the point in the journey where you use the resources available to you to understand how to resolve the problems you are currently faced with.

Growing up, one constant theme I remember is freedom. Always understanding the consequences of each choice I made, even something as simple as a bedtime. My mother would give me her recommended bedtime and reasoning behind it, and if I poorly managed my time I paid the price in the morning. If I waited until Sunday evening to do my homework and something fun came up, I couldn't participate because of homework. As an adult, I've been able to apply those very lessons of balancing freedom and it's consequences. So many people question how I'm able to complete my master's program online. Well, that's how. It's what works for me!

Dealing with the Past

Growing up I never felt good enough, even though I had every reason to feel good about myself. I was always at the top of my class academically, very talented in any activity I tried, and very beautiful. Yet it was never enough. As the first born of a single mother, my mom learned a lot on the go with me. She's always been my rock, and I'm forever thankful for that! But in an attempt to create a spirit of excellence she created an environment where perfection seemed like the only option. That combined with my experiences with my father led to me to the belief that I was not good enough.

I've always known exactly who my father was, which is more than some can say. Growing up, my relationship with him taught me that if things got too difficult for him to be a father to me, he'd go away. Which left me feeling like I'm not worth fighting for. Now in my teen and adult years I've begun to push people away to see if they are going to leave because I feel that's the only way I can control their inevitable exit.

All of that combined has brought me to a feeling of self-loathing and not self-love, something I never realized until this past month. Scary right? How do you live through 23 years of life and not love yourself? Who knew that was even possible? The important part now is that I plan on fixing it! Which leaves me with this question: How exactly do you fall in love with yourself?

God

Why I need Him

Atelophobia is the fear of not being good enough. Who knows if that's the true term for it, but that fear is 100% real. The feeling of not being good enough or being just good enough to get by is something I've experienced my entire life. Feeling like you're never going to get the true desires of your heart is a tough feeling. The toughest part is trying to figure out what to do after yet another failure. I find solace in knowing there are so many successful people who started as failures, but eventually become success stories. I just hope one day I can be my own success story.

Having faith in God requires a consistent level of faith and trust even in the face of failure and life's many challenges. I have to continue to believe that everything happens for a reason, even when that reason seems impossible to understand. I have to continue to believe that

God will never leave my side, nor will he neglect my needs and desires.

He is my father and I am His child. God will never put more on you than you can bare, and I am living proof! Let me pause here for a moment and explain what I think that concept means. Nothing comes into our lives (good, bad, or ugly) that God doesn't approve. This doesn't mean he is the author of everything that happens to us, but that means he has to allow it to impact us. I find comfort in that knowing that if God allowed me to go through it, he knows I can make it to the other side! And if God, who knows everything about me and my challenge, says I can win the battle then I can!

Growing through Him

A challenge of my growth and development is applying that knowledge to my own life. Just like the other challenges I've faced recently, I plan to pass this one. I'm going to stay focused and motivated on working towards my dreams. I've finally found my true passion, and I plan to fight for it. One of my favorite poems is "Don't Quit" with the most applicable part being, "when your funds are low and your debts are high. When you're laughing although you'd rather cry". Even if I have to recite this poem every day of my life, I cannot and will not quit.

God promised he'd give me the desires of my heart and I'm putting my faith in him to do just that. Maybe God is simply testing my faith and dedication prior to allowing me to experience my breakthrough. Either way I will continue to apply my best efforts and have faith that He will see me through. I truly believe He would not put (or allow) these desires into my heart to tease me, and because of that faith I will continue to push forward. In the end, I know my efforts will be rewarded.

The topic of faith is heavy on my heart this morning. Today is Sunday and although I haven't been to church in months, which I am very disappointed about, my faith has remained un-waivered. My biggest concern is why haven't I gone to church in so long? It's really concerning, because I have no clue as to why. Maybe I should continue looking for a new church? I'm truly not sure. However, this week my faith faced a huge test! Just as I felt like things were falling into place, I got news of a huge set back. My immediate thought was "if it's meant to happen

God will make a way, if not maybe it's too soon." The beauty is that I meant that response with all of my heart.

I'm learning to truly trust in God's timing with an understanding that when He feels I'm ready then it will happen. Over time it becomes tough for everything to be in a transitional period for so long. I try to hold onto to my faith by knowing my perseverance will be rewarded when this transitional period is finally over! Having comfort in that allows me to push through even the darkest of days.

A Mother's Love

Lately I've been more aware of how critical my mother is in my life! I've come to the realization that God speaks to me DIRECTLY through her. For years I felt frustrated because I never felt like I heard from God. I didn't feel like I could hear His voice; I now see that He was talking to me through her. She gave me a CD recording of the sermon my pastor preached yesterday. Listening to it reminded me of how much I miss my home church since moving down south, spiritually. I've decided to start watching services from my home church via online broadcasting since I haven't found a church that can feed my soul in the same way down south.

When talking with my mom last night she mentioned that God will often speak to a man through his wife. To me this means that I need to get back right with God. I need to be in a position to be a benefit to my husband in this manner. I've always wanted to be a mother and wife, and at some point it may have been all I wanted. At this point, I can honestly be thankful that it hasn't happened yet. The person I now see myself becoming will be a much healthier, happier, and stronger person for my family. I don't know when God intends for me to have a family of my own, but I know it will happen in due time. Additionally, I know they will be proud of the person they will know. In the meantime I have so much that I want to accomplish in life and I'm working towards those goals.

Growing Pains

I've learned that when I pray and ask God for something I have to be prepared to handle above and beyond what I expected. I also learned to be careful not to complain about what I asked for. Crazy thought, right? I asked God to turn my financial situation around, and his response was giving me more hours at work. Who am I to then turn around and complain about being tired? It's completely ridiculous. So learning to be happy with the answer to my prayers is key!

I recently watched a sermon online, from my home church, and it was extremely powerful to me, even though I had seen it before. In the message I took away a few key points:

1. I need to close the doors on my sins and unhealthy relationships.

2. I need to pour into others, and stop minimizing what I have to give.

3. The key to receiving my blessings starts with obedience to God.

These points hit home for me because they really opened my eyes to how backwards I was acting. How dare I pray for financial stability when I haven't paid my tithes in SEVERAL months? How dare I pray for a healthy relationship when I'm still entertaining unhealthy relationships from the past? It's just completely and utterly backwards to the point that I'm truly embarrassed.

The beauty with God is that He is a forgiving God. Crazy enough, as I wrote that I had to check myself. I had assumed His forgiveness without even asking for it. I stopped mid sentence and prayed for the forgiveness I'd assumed He had already given me. Being the Christian woman that I want to become isn't going to be easy, but I am officially including it as a part of my active growth plan. I'm requiring it of myself to be better, because the reality is that without God I'm truly nothing. It amazes me how people can live life without knowing that, but I guess everyone needs to learn that in his or her own special way. It is my goal to watch a sermon everyday through the end of the month. I am restarting my lifestyle diet and requiring this to be a part of it. I'm eager to see how my life will be impacted. If after one day my heart has already changed so much, I'm eager to watch the next day's lesson.

Since starting to take a more active approach to my relationship with God, I can see a serious change in my life. I start my mornings by watching a sermon online. I find myself in such a great mood, I'm learning different areas I need to improve spiritually, and I feel much closer to God. Literally I wake up anxious to see what my lesson for the day is. The bible says, "Draw near to God and He will draw near to you." (James 4:8). I completely feel this happening for me!

Learning to let go and give my concerns to God is probably the most difficult thing I've had to learn to date. Yet I know things become so much easier when you allow God to sit in the driver seat. Sometimes the fear of the unknown becomes crippling, but fear is the kryptonite to prayer. If I'm praying for something, being anxious or fearful cancels out that prayer. With the struggles of life, sometimes fear is a natural reaction. Being able to snap myself out of the thoughts of fear and stand strong in the word of God is key!

My life has been full of struggles this past year, but I feel myself growing as a result of those struggles. As I look back on the progress I've made it truly makes me proud. I know that it'll all be worth it in the long run. For that reason I continue to push through! Trying to figure out what my next steps in life should be has been a very confusing process. Sometimes waiting to hear God's response gets confusing as well, but often times I have to remind myself that asking God for clarity is okay.

Clarity with regards to my career, friendships, and relationships is necessary. Most importantly, understanding how to create a permanent solution to my financial struggles is necessary. While I've learned a lot over the past year or so, it's been a serious struggle. I'm currently at a place where there's nothing else I can do to improve my financial situation. At this point I've learned that I have to give all control up to God. I'm literally doing all that I can and from here it's in God's hands.

I have continued to focus on my spiritual growth and development while challenging myself to focus on my physical growth, ensuring that I'm not only committing to daily online bible study but also applying those lessons to my life. My current growth exercise, and in my opinion is the most important one, is learning to trust God completely. The concept of "let go and let God" is something that rolls off the tongue with ease, but learning to fully place God in the driver's seat of your entire life is not so easy a task.

I say it's the most important lesson because it's a fundamental piece of being a Christian. It requires me to trust God and have faith in His plan for my life, and I'm learning that my plans may not be the best for me. This is one of the most difficult things I've had to do. In all efforts to give God control over my life it's been worth it. He's shown Himself strong in my life, and for that I am thankful.

To make those efforts towards giving God control, I have to first ask Him for direction and clarity, and I have to learn to be okay with His answer even if it's different from what I had in mind. Even so, being completely willing to go wherever He wants me to go is the challenge. Since I'm such a strong willed person and free spirit that's not always the easiest thing for me to do. Learning to adjust my desires to match God's desires and truly being okay with whatever direction He's sending me is what I'm working on.

At times that's truly the most difficult thing for me, especially with my financial situation lately. Things have been getting increasingly difficult, despite me working my butt off, and my bank accounts are consistently in the negative. What am I supposed to do? I literally have nothing else I can do except trust God to handle things.

I find myself getting extremely stressed out, and I'm honestly not sure what I can do to productively solve this problem. My #1 cause of stress is my very limited income. I'm reaching a place of complete frustration and I'm not sure how things will work out. I'm trying my best to trust God, but this has certainly been a test. When my finances are out of order it makes life seem so much more stressful. So much in life requires money that when you don't have it your stress becomes elevated. Every month for the past year I've had to worry or stress over my financial situation, with no sign of a breakthrough, despite me urgently needing and praying for one.

Repentance & Forgiveness

My biggest area of struggle is around sexual sin. Not only sex outside of marriage, but being attracted to women. The Bible clearly states homosexuality is an abomination and those who are of that lifestyle will not inherit the kingdom of God. How do I then rid myself of something that comes to me so naturally? For me, sex is an important part of life, but I have to find a way to stop living (comfortably) in sin. Overtime I have embraced this lifestyle of sin as if it was okay, choosing to make my wrongs somehow become right.

To be a Christian it requires a lifestyle of repentance. That means it is a constant act, not just a one-time repentance. And to repent means to feel remorseful AND turn away from doing it again. That's not necessarily an easy thing to do, but the bible promises, "Resist the devil, and he will flee from you" (James 4:7). I believe in the promise that God will protect me if I trust him!

This morning my sermon/lesson was on the subject of forgiveness. It's such a difficult thing to give, yet we expect to receive it from others and especially from God freely and frequently. Often times we don't even ask for forgiveness but we expect it to happen. It is often misunderstood that forgiveness is about releasing others from guilt, when in reality it's about releasing the pain and bitterness from our own hearts. It's important to forgive people who've hurt us regardless of if they have asked for forgiveness or deserve it.

The difficult part for me comes when I factor in the pain my father has caused over the years. How do I move past the pain he's caused to truly let that pain go COMPLETELY? The sermon this morning brought up several points. The first point was a challenge to look past the pain or the person to find the purpose for that pain. I understand that God allowed the pain into my life for a reason, likely with the purpose of growth.

I also came to the realization that God constantly forgives me when I make mistakes, even when I haven't repented, so how can I expect that of God but have zero willingness to do the same for others? I think genuine forgiveness is going to be key for a successful relationship. Being able to let it go and move on when my partner has hurt, disappointed, or even neglected me, and vice versa. No one is perfect and understanding that mistakes do happen is going to be key! Maybe in time, with applied effort, I will be able to move past the pain experienced by a critical relationship in my life. I pray that God softens my heart so that I'm able to grow to have a relationship with my father.

Additionally, when I have children I do not want my pain to spill over into their connection and relationship. It wouldn't be fair to keep my children from their grand parent because of my past hurt. It also wouldn't be fair to subject my children to the same pain, when it's my job to protect them. I'm praying for wisdom and a heart of forgiveness. It is my desire to grow past the pain of my past.

Quiet Time w/ God

I've decided for a week prior to my birthday I was going to fast with prayer focused on my financial stability. No social media, TV, eating out, or outgoing communication. I plan to take this time to hear from God what He has planned for my life to bring about permanent financial stability. Although it is a short time to be fasting, I know it'll be a challenge for me. I am calling on God and depending on Him to make a way. Throughout this fast I will center my prayers on financial stability and apply my attention and effort around the things I can control, allowing God to handle the things I cannot control. He has to make a way because He promised to never leave or forsake me.

That brings up a very profound realization for me. The words "forsake" means to abandon, and if I am to believe in such a core principle of the Christian faith, how is it possible for me to have abandonment issues? The most necessary person in my life made a written promise to never abandon me. Shouldn't that be good enough to hold onto? From that perspective is it even worth my time to be concerned about a friend, dating interest, or even a family member abandoning me? Not at all! I will make genuine efforts to keep that in mind the next time the fear of abandonment creeps into my heart. The key will be to identify it early enough and prevent this feeling from surfacing.

So often I feel so lost in life and it becomes extremely difficult for me to see clearly the direction I should be going, especially with me trying to follow God's will. The question very frequently becomes, "God what is your will?" I think this fast will be beneficial because it will help to remove other sources of information, allowing for clarity from God. Which may have been a large part of the problem of why I can't hear from Him. How am I supposed to hear God's answer when I'm looking at too many sources for the answer? No wonder I feel so lost.

23 ...and Finally Loving Me

The reality is that 99% of those on my social media do not have a genuine interest or investment in my life. Maybe 95% because Facebook has some family members who I know care, but a large majority do not care and attempting to gain attention through social media is unhealthy. Why would people reach out to check on me when they get a play by play through social media? At that point what else is left to talk about? They've already gotten their updates on their newsfeed. I'd be interested to see what happens when I don't post my life.

I swear as much as I grow there's still much more growth for me to experience. It feels like every day there's something new for me to work on. I wish for the day where my developmental work will be done, but that's not likely to happen until I'm in heaven. I am simply hoping to continue to grow closer to the woman God has destined for me to become.

Me

Challenging growth

I am honestly living through the concept of "growing pains". My hope is that by my 24th birthday I will be in a truly happy place in life. I pray that things in my life continue to grow and progress in the correct direction. These directions include professionally, personally, emotionally, spiritually, financially, and just an overall well-being. That's my prayer.

A revelation I received from a talk with my mother is that I should look into finding a therapist. My only drawback is the frustration of spending weeks or even months doing long-winded assessments and not making progress towards my real issues. There is the upside that I might meet the correct therapist and have a breakthrough. I had a therapist my last year of college and it was an amazing therapeutic connection. We made a lot of progress and things were starting to workout, and most importantly I was gaining a deeper understanding of myself. I really hope that I'm able to find a therapist who can help me work through my problems. I want to learn how to do better and experience a better way of life.

The biggest goal I have for the coming year is buying my first home! Every time I think about it, I get excited. I've rented for years (money wasted) primarily because I wanted the freedom to move. Now that I'm living down south, I'm truly happy and look forward to planting my roots here. I look forward to hosting holiday parties and inviting my family to stay and visit. I think I might even try to host Thanksgiving...oh boy! Most importantly, to be able to have a home to call my own, that's my dream. Not to mention money paid in rent does absolutely nothing for you; it's pretty much a waste of money. When paying a mortgage, which is usually cheaper than renting, the money is going towards your financial value and working to build your worth. One of my biggest goals in life is ownership in homes, businesses, and in the things that impact my everyday life.

Some of my other goals for this year include traveling more and reading more. I want to plan a trip outside the country for my 24th birthday as well. It would be nice to visit a new culture to celebrate my life. For now I'm going to do what I can to achieve those goals. Self-improvement is a daily process and I have to make daily, consistent, and conscious efforts towards my goals. One day I will be that much closer to touching the fruits of my labor, and I'm keeping in mind that "progress is a slow process."

Self-Care

Lately I've been really struggling in life and feeling like a failure. It's hard to learn how to love yourself and be confident in whom you are when you keep failing. I think with this year approaching, I'm going to get myself a memory jar. I'm going to document my happy moments, and when things get tough I will review all the good in my life. I have to find a way to spend more time focusing on my victories and learning from the failures instead of allowing the failures to get me down about life.

Maybe reading through my journal and looking specifically for the good moments will help me feel better about life overall. I've learned that, for me, when things are going bad it's hard for me to see the good, which creates this cycle of constant struggle. My therapist in college brought to my attention that I have borderline personality disorder. The clearest way she described it is that my emotions are often triggered by some event in my life, whether good or bad, and often times when a major event happens it impacts the lens I see the world through. So when things are good I often only notice good things in my life, but when things are bad that's all I'm able to see. Under that context, I'm hoping this memory jar will help me to adjust the lens through which I see my world.

I am co-chairing an event for my sorority and the topic I am responsible for is self-esteem, positive self-image, and/or choosing me. The event is for young girls, but preparing my portion will inevitably help me as well. I'm very much looking forward to learning and growing as a part of preparing to help young girls grow and develop. It's funny how helping others will allow you to help yourself as well!

Sometimes it gets me down when I think about how I don't love myself and how I should've learned that lesson 15+ years ago. I realize that I can't do anything about the past; all I can do is continue to move forward. After all, life isn't about finding yourself; it's about creating yourself. I've very much enjoyed the time I've taken to get to know myself and to explore what truly makes me happy. I still have a long way to go and so much more to explore, but I've begun the journey towards happiness!

Love! What a powerful drug! For the first time in my life I'm looking internally for love and finding out it's truly enough. And with the growing love that I have for myself, my overall life experience has improved. I couldn't possibly sit here and imply that things have been perfect because they haven't. Things have been rough these past few months, yet I still feel happy overall. Sometimes I sit back and wonder why.

I've learned to focus my energy on things I have control over and put everything else in God's hands. There are times when I get overwhelmed with the rough patches, but when I am able to refocus myself the burdens feel much lighter. Through this approach to life, my life seems to be going smoother. I've learned that I can't change the events of my life, but I can change how I react to those events. It's my prayer that anyone reading this book is able to grow and develop into a better version of themselves. Although my journey towards active growth has only been a few months, my outlook on life has changed drastically.

Self-confidence can be a very tricky thing. Often people are inaccurately assumed to have confidence in themselves and they may even appear to. For me, I assumed I had high self-esteem until one day I realized it was only at the surface. I thought I loved myself until age 23. Can you imagine how tough of a pill that is to swallow that you don't love yourself? But as difficult as it was to accept, it was a necessary evil.

For me, learning to love myself started with getting to know who I truly am. After breaking up with my ex I really had to evaluate who I was as an adult. Prior to this evaluation, I had made a large majority of my adult decisions while factoring him in. I would put aside my hopes, dreams, and desires to benefit our relationship. If I wanted to do this or that and he didn't...we didn't. For me a chance at marriage was well worth the sacrifices I made. After our breakup I had to take the time to learn what I liked, what I wanted, and what made me truly happy.

Additionally, I needed to create goals for myself that didn't depend on someone else. I needed to find my own dreams and aspirations to focus on. Prior to the break up my only goals were to be a mother and wife. And while those are such beautiful goals, I now want so much more. But the most difficult part was learning how to love myself after 23 years. How do you start that process after so many years? It took me deciding what I was worth and standing strong in that. I have been monitoring how I allow people to treat me and standing up for myself, which is key.

I've come to understand that the reason I had so many one-sided friendships was because that's what I allowed. I've learned to see that my dating life was as bad as it was because I taught guys it was okay to treat me that way. I was so desperate to have a boyfriend and close friends that I accepted anything from anyone willing. I had to learn to be okay alone in order to realize that being alone was better than being treated like an option. Now, those that I'm closet to are actually making an effort to be in my life and they deserve to be in my life. I have standards, and I protect them.

Being a naturally giving person is tough at times, because we live in a world where givers get taken. I had to find a way to protect myself. Learning the most effective way to protect myself has been challenging to say the least. In middle school I decided being rude to people was the most effective way to protect myself. I rationalized that if I was rude to people they would hesitate to ask me for anything. And, because I don't know how to say no, that was the safer option for me. I held onto that mindset until two years ago. After embracing that mindset for about 10 years, you can imagine it was difficult to break out of, but I had a wake up call and decided to change for the better. So I eventually moved away from the angry black woman persona. Sometimes I slip back into that mindset easier than I'd like to, but ultimately I've grown a lot since then and I'm very proud of that!

New Beginnings

New Year's Day symbolizes new beginnings and honestly I'm completely excited about it! I feel that I've been planting seeds over the last few months that will begin to blossom within the next few months. For some reason our culture has glamorized the idea of New Year's resolutions, and while I encourage growth and making positive changes, why wait until a new year? The reality is that most New Year's resolutions are short lived. Self-improvement should be a daily process! If you're serious about change, the date won't matter because it will require daily effort anyway.

At this point I can accurately attest to the fact that change is not easy, but I'm also prepared to attest to it being worth it! I've grown so much and there's still so much more to do, but it's helped me enjoy life more and experience true and genuine happiness. For me, true happiness means being in love with myself, having the freedom to do what my heart desires, and experiencing growth. Part of loving myself means having true self-confidence, being able to provide self-validation, enjoying my solitude, and being the truest version of myself. One thing I've learned to do is to protect my peace and put my happiness first (okay that's two). I truly feel putting my happiness first is the hardest, yet it is the most important thing I'll ever need to do. It's important to find a balance between being the naturally giving person I am and learning when I need to be selfish. If I don't put my happiness first, then who will?

Right now my church is focused on teaching ways to living a great life in order to make the rest of my days the best of my life. Between the book, church, and therapy I am in a position to receive the necessary tools to move to the next step! I've always appreciated the concept of therapy. After a few unproductive therapy relationships I'd begun to get frustrated with the process of finding the right therapist. Recently I've decided to take the risk and search for a new therapist. After one appointment I feel good about our connection. For whatever reason there is a stigma that only crazy people seek counseling, but I truly feel that if you wait until you've completely lost your mind you've waited until it's too late! Therapy is beneficial when dealing with the life problems we all have and can help provide clarity, guidance, and help to work through the pain.

It's been almost a year since I've moved down south, and really the past year of my life has been such a transitional period. It has not been an easy one to say the least, and essentially my entire life has been flipped upside down. I hope things end up smoothing out soon because it's been a very stressful time for me. From the move down south, ending things with my ex, to work stress, career transitions, and personal growth. I'm beginning to grow tired of having things be so uncertain.

Emotional Growth

Personally, I truly feel it is okay to cry. The catch is that I will only allow myself one time to cry over the same reason...then never again. I think it's important to allow yourself to feel your emotions and learn to process them. We as humans naturally feel emotions, but are sometimes taught not to show or express them. While being overly emotional may be dangerous, having a balanced amount of emotion is healthy. I've learned that the main difference is whether or not you allow your emotions to control your actions.

It's okay that the rude clerk made you mad, but it's not okay to lower your ethical standards and be rude in return. It's okay that the love of your life disappointed you, but it's not okay to overreact by cursing, yelling, and screaming...or worse. Sometimes your boss will frustrate you, but is it worth allowing them to ruin your day because of it? Let me pause here for a second and share my own life lesson regarding my anger and attitude.

I used to quickly turn to anger and constantly responded to conflict with attitude. It was bad enough that my boyfriend at the time was embarrassed to be in public with me; it was then that I realized I needed to change. I had to learn that cursing, yelling, and carrying around a bad attitude was not the way to get what I wanted from someone. It only made me look stupid and furthered the "angry black woman" stereotype. Now, when I see women acting as I would've, I chuckle, but I truly hope they learn how peaceful life can be if only they checked themselves first.

Now I make efforts towards being pleasant just because. If someone rubs me the wrong way, I find a way to communicate without reciprocating the anger or I just ignore it. I don't let people treat me disrespectfully, but I don't treat them poorly either. It hasn't been an easy road towards improving my attitude, but it's been worth it. My biggest improvement has been my ability to deal with people in the retail and service industries. As someone who worked most of my life in retail I understand that no one wants to deal with "that" customer, but when you get a customer who is refreshingly pleasant, it's a breath of fresh air. I now make an effort to be the pleasant customer.

The reality is the store associates usually want to help you and are more than willing to go the extra mile for you when they like you. Suddenly that rule gets a little more flexible. Even when the store associate can't do anything for you, you've done something for them. You've brightened their day and made their shift that much more bearable, which should ultimately feel good to you. I'm learning to positively reinforce the good I experience instead of negatively reinforcing the bad. I choose to make an effort to acknowledge and show appreciation for the good interactions I have with others. By focusing on the good and giving off good vibes, I've found that I attract more good to me.

Me Time!

It has been said that God answers prayers three ways: "yes", "not now", or "I have something better in store" and I truly believe that! I also believe that what may seem like God's "no" is actually him protecting me from something or someone. When it comes to dating, it can become difficult to understand and apply the wisdom of God's answer. As I try to apply His wisdom in every other area of my life, I must also do so in my dating life. Although I miss companionship, maybe God is telling me I'm not ready yet. Maybe my future husband is not ready yet, but I trust that the wait will be worth it.

If I'm being honest with myself, I feel like my life is a mess. Maybe I don't have the emotional and mental space to allow someone into my life right now, and I think I'm okay with that. In the meantime I have plenty else to focus my time, energy, and attention on. I should be focusing on school, starting my new career, and focusing on my family. Additionally, I am focusing on being a more involved member of my sorority. Until things begin to improve in these areas of life, I just shouldn't even be focused on my dating life.

Tiara Riley

Yesterday I had the thought, if I'm there for everyone...who's going to be there for me? If I wrote a list of everyone's life and/or problems I help, I question who's going to do the same for me? Who can I vent to or share my life with? I guess me? Writing really does help me to vent and release the inner feelings that might otherwise be kept bottled in. Writing also helps me get clarity when I am going through things. It's funny how I love to write but I have to force myself to read books! The book I'm reading now is pretty good! It's called "The Woman Code" and basically the author talks about how to reprogram your internal code in order to live a happy and fulfilling life. The book is full of healthy and relevant challenges to my perspective in life, which is needed!

Personally, I'm someone who needs balance and consistency. Not having balance or consistency for the past year or so has been very tough on my spirit. I keep hoping things will start to get better, but so far they don't seem to be. Sometimes I have to wonder if it's a question of my perspective, but I really don't think so. This transition period has simply just been tough.

Progress

One area that I'm finally starting to see results in is the area of my personal growth. I can finally look back and see that I have made a lot of progress. I've been able to see myself handle things differently than I would've a year ago, and that brings me great confirmation. Although I know I have a lot more work to do on myself, I can at least acknowledge that I'm nowhere near the old me. I look forward to seeing how much I will have grown over the next year as well. Even over the next 5 years, that should be a beautiful sight to see.

Over the past year I've grown a lot and I can truly say that I am proud of my growth. I have gotten to know myself, created goals for myself, and my future, and learned to raise my standards. I have taken conscious and active steps towards growth and development. Although it has been a very challenging year, I have continued to push through it. The crazy part about looking at how far my growth has come along is looking at how far I still have to go. I firmly believe the person I was a year ago has changed so much for the better. I have become happier by removing the people and things in life that took away from that happiness. I have become healthier emotionally and mentally by learning how to address life's challenges.

My favorite part about this past year has been my ability to find goals I'm passionate about other than starting a family. I spent two decades of my life being passionate about two things: marriage and kids, which is a goal that requires another willing individual. The past 12 months have been the most challenging months of my life, but it is my prayer that the growth that has occurred as a result of the many challenges will be worth it. I fully understand that God has been preparing me for the things that I have asked Him for. I have stayed strong, I have persevered, and I have learned at every opportunity possible. I truly believe that God will reward me for my efforts.

Until then I will continue to grow, develop, and find areas for self-improvement. I know that one day I will look back and be thankful that I had the courage to push through all of life's obstacles I'm currently facing. Even now, I'm already thankful even before seeing the reward. For the first time in my life I am proud of myself, and I also finally know what genuine happiness feels like. I have also learned to protect my peace and happiness.

To date the biggest lesson I've learned is how to teach people how to treat me. I have learned without a shadow of a doubt that people treat you how you allow them to treat you. I used to be so afraid for people to leave my life that I would allow them to dictate my role in their life. If I said I wanted a relationship and a guy said he didn't, I would still have sex with them because I thought that was better than nothing. I now have the strength, courage, and respect for myself to know that I deserve more.

Over this past year I have also learned how to enjoy the peacefulness of alone time, allowing myself time to recover from daily interactions with people. I am learning that being alone is not a punishment, but a reward. I am also coming to the realization that it is okay to do things by myself as well. While I'm excited about the growth I have made, I'm most excited about the growth in my future. Everyday I get closer to becoming the woman I aspire to be, and in due time I know I can and will get there. I don't have to be running as long as I'm consistently moving in the right direction.

Tiara Riley

Things in life have been quite confusing, but I've been making a genuine effort to trust God and take life one day at a time. Things have been going well, but not because my problems have been resolved. I truly feel God's peace over my heart! Everyday I've been working towards my goals and preparing myself to achieve them. It's not been easy, but I stand firm that it'll be worth it! I am fighting for the future of my dreams!

I have felt progress in the friendships I have. I've felt closer to some, okay with the distance of others, and I'm feeling more comfortable developing new friendships. Being able to develop and foster my existing friendships has been key. I've also been making a genuine effort towards enjoying my youth. I've been doing so by finding the time and money to get out and enjoy life as much as possible. Even though I work a lot, my schedule is not too hectic that I can't have fun. I make time for who and what is important to me; I'm just making sure I place myself at the top of that list. The reality is, if I'm not taking care of myself, who else is going to?

23 ...and Finally Loving Me

Feeling that people take advantage of my giving heart has been a concern throughout my life. What I've learned to do is to keep those with similar hearts close, and keep people who take advantage of me at a distance. Following that method of protection has been effective for me. It has created a healthy and safe environment for me to be myself. I don't have to be rude in order to protect myself, as I thought was necessary growing up. I don't have to change the person I am at my core; I just have to keep the right people around me. When I look back on how much I've grown, it's such a beautiful thing. Sometimes I focus so much on the growth I have ahead of me that I don't realize how much more growth I have already done.

Earlier this week I felt myself getting really down about feeling a sense of frustration. I was feeling very frustrated that life seems to be at a standstill and my efforts towards progress were feeling futile. What happened afterwards was probably one of the most critical things for my growth. At the suggestion of my mother, I decided to look through my journals over the past year and see my progress. Taking the time to do this allowed me to see quite a bit.

For starters I was able to see some progress and breakthroughs. I could see my growth as well as the answers to the very prayers I had. It was nice to be able to remind myself that God does hear my prayers and he answers them when I'm ready. I was also able to see that in the areas of my biggest frustration I'd been the most inconsistent. The only thing I'd do on a consistent basis was complain about those problems and get frustrated. Well, at this point enough is enough!

I'm finally going to map out a game plan for all areas of my life that I'm able to stick to. I'm going to commit to realistic goals and work on keeping them as a consistent focus. In reading through the journals I got really upset with myself because I was able to see the patterns of inconsistency. But I can't change the past; I can only use the lessons of the past to create a better future for myself.

Today I'm locking myself in my room and spending alone time with God. No TV, phone, music, not even a sense of time. My goal for this alone time is to reset and connect with God to see His direction for my life. I feel like I'm reaching a place of spiritual maturity where I want Him to control my life. Learning to give Him control is my current growth challenge. Spending this alone time with God is my first step in that direction.

Looking back on the last year so much has changed and I'm so beyond thankful for the growth I've experienced. I had some very key goals for this year and I think they're coming along. The most important goal for this year was to learn to love myself. In order to do this I had to first get to know myself. I needed to fully understand who I am, what makes me happy, and what I want in life. After gaining a true and deep understanding of myself, it became easy to love me. Now that I love myself, I've created the opportunity for someone else to love me. I am now in a position to experience love as it was intended to be experienced! What a beautiful thing!

My dating life has been going pretty well lately and seems to be improving everyday. I'm very excited to see how things continue to progress and thankful for what I have experienced so far. My biggest challenge has been learning to control the pace of my emotional development while dating. Learning to manage the pace so that I can develop and maintain a healthy connection. I've also been slowly learning how to let a man lead in the relationship and how to fully trust someone with my heart. That has proven to be a slow and complicated lesson.

My next biggest goal of the year was to place a constant focus on my growth and development. I have grown emotionally, mentally, and spiritually. Financial and physical growths are still on my radar, but I've seen some struggle in these areas. I'm very proud of my mental and emotional growth, but I'm most proud of my spiritual growth. I have finally decided to have a personal relationship with God for myself.

Granted I grew up very active in the church and even a regular attendee as an adult, but I have transitioned from being religious to having a genuine relationship with God. Learning to apply the principles taught in the Bible to my daily life has made the biggest difference. Allowing God to call the shots in my life has been a tough lesson to learn. But the more I allow Him to control my life, the less stress and worry I experience. And God has helped me to uncover my true destiny...one step at a time.

My final primary focus for the year was about experiencing everything my heart desires and finding my true happiness. While I have learned to find true happiness, which came as a part of emotional growth, I haven't had the time or money to experience everything my heart desires. I'm hoping to be able to do so this in the coming year! As my 24th birthday approaches I think I want to put life experiences, consistent workouts, and financial growth as my primary focuses for the year of 24!

The Big 2-4

As my birthday month arrives, for me that means an official start to countdown to my birthday. I'm very much looking forward to celebrating turning 24 and being able to acknowledge my growth over this past year. I have vacation time from my part time job and it's my intent to use that time to pack up my house. I will also be planning to be able to walk away from that part time job. I have several streams of income I'm attempting to get going to be able to sustain myself long term.

My biggest goal currently is to be looking towards the start of my first business. It has not been easy, but I have faith that this is where I should be taking my next steps and it'll be worth it! I'm practicing patience, hard work, and perseverance while understanding progress is a slow process. Going through this process has been a testament to my growth and development. In the past, if something was too difficult or took too long, I would give up and lose interest. But this is something I'm willing, ready, and able to work for, making it that much more precious to me.

I have a couple more potential income streams that'll serve as supplemental income for me as well. Learning to create multiple sources of income, in my opinion, is a critical part of becoming an entrepreneur. Being an entrepreneur is not easy and is very much unpredictable. Having several sources of income will allow me to create some sense of financial security for me. That's going to put me in a much healthier place.

Personally, I tend to get frustrated with myself when I feel like I should be further along in life than I am. But the more I improve in that area, the better and more stress free life becomes. "Let go and let God" has become more than a mantra, but a way of life for me. Things tend to get the most frustrating when I realize I don't own my home, I'm not established in my career, and I'm not married. I've done some research on those life decisions. According to Google, women get married on average at age 27 and men at 29. First home purchases happen around age 31 on average, and the average age of having their first child is 25. So, according to those averages, I have plenty of time and I'm ahead of schedule.

I'm finally starting to get excited about my upcoming birthday! It's about six days until I am 24. It's been a rough year to say the least, but all in all I'm thankful for the year of growth. I'm truly proud of how far I've come along. I've not grown completely, but that's an unrealistic goal. I have learned so much about myself, and that has allowed me to embrace the good and work to improve the bad. I have learned to be less extreme and find a healthy balance in my challenges. Most importantly I have learned to love myself. This year did not turn out at all how I hoped it would've, but part of my growth process is to be more forgiving of myself and learn to roll with the punches more often. Being not as hard on myself without losing my ability to hold myself accountable has been my challenge.

My prayer is that this year has served as preparation for the life I dream of, and that I can begin to experience that life every step of the way. I'm praying for stability and joy throughout this next year and to continue to grow for life. I pray for stability in my finances, my dating life, and with friends and family. I pray for consistency in my walk with God and my commitment to working out. This upcoming year my primary focuses will be on continuing my spiritual growth, committing to an active lifestyle, and financial growth. My goal professionally is to start my first business and create multiple sources of income for myself.

Fitness will become a higher priority for me and I will find a way to push myself to be consistent. Not only consistent workouts, but to monitor what I'm eating as well. There are some people who really enjoy working out, but I simply enjoy the results. Maybe then results are what I should be focusing on. Spiritually I have grown A LOT! And that's what I'm most proud of. My goal is to continue to grow as a Christian, deepen my walk with God, and learn to depend on Him more and more each day.

Finding my Voice

But Who Cares?

Throughout my life I've always felt that my voice had little to no value, which I guess can go back to a longing need for validation. When deciding to write this book, I asked myself on several occasions "What if no one ever reads it?" and I came to the realization that my opinion still matters. Learning to accept this concept is one step in the journey towards self-love and finding value in myself. I've always had a different way of thinking, but at times our society shuns that, especially being a young adult! We're taught by society to stick to the status quo because being safe is better than any other choice.

We're taught to go to school, get good grades, go to college (while racking up student loans), don't forget grad school because a Bachelor's degree is no longer good enough, then find a 9-5 job, and pretend to be fulfilled in it. I challenge anyone reading this, even if it is one person, to do what you want to do and be willing to take a leap of faith to get there. I think too many people get so caught up in the need for a steady flow of income that they're afraid to take calculated risks for the sake of true job satisfaction.

Every time I go to write in this book, I question if anyone will ever read it but I've had to remind myself that my voice is valuable. Even if no one is around to hear it, a tree falling in the woods still makes a sound. I think we're raised as a society to follow the status quo and that just doesn't work for me. I saw something today that said, "The more you love your decisions, the less you need others to". This hit home so hard because it's exactly what my growth and transition is all about right now. The more I go through my growing process, the more I learn to enjoy life. And although I'm in a transitional process, I truly feel that within the next few months I will have everything I want/desire.

I find myself writing in my journal more often than I write in this book. I often question why and I think it's a mix between wondering what I should talk about, questioning the validity of my voice, and my attention starting to fade. I keep in mind that completing this book would be a great accomplishment for me. Several times throughout life I have started books, usually fictional, and never completed them. Sometimes I wish I didn't have such a short attention span, but maybe I can just learn to best manage it. My short attention span has been impacting many areas of my life including my career aspirations, my dating interests, and things that I want to do in life. The challenge now becomes how to adjust my flaw so that it becomes my strength.

Writing this book has been a consistent struggle throughout the year, but a large part of this journey is finding the value of my voice. With that being said, I'm recommitting to the cause. Although I'm not letting anyone read it until it's done, anyone who has been told about it seems to think it's a good idea. I was talking to a friend of mine who confirmed the importance of the POV and the growth experience of this year of life.

So much emphasis is on the partying and freedom of age 21 and when you hit age 25 you realize how close you are to age 30. A lot of time, by age 30 we are expected to be fully established in life, but how do you get to that place in life? How do you find yourself and begin to establish yourself in life? I think the first step involves learning what is important to me and working towards achieving that. For me, it also involves getting to know and learning to love me. Going after the desires of my heart is easy for me, but I understand that it can be challenging for some.

Embracing the Process

I feel so refreshed in life. It's such a new place for me to decide to focus on my happiness. It was my norm to give of myself and focus on putting others first. I put the happiness of those I'm closest to as a priority, particularly when I was in my last relationship. Learning to find myself and asking the question "who are you?" have been some of the best things I could've done. Because I'm getting to know myself better I'm able to genuinely enjoy falling in love with myself, and so far so good.

One important part of my development process has been open and honest feedback from those in my life. Between friends, family, and even an ex-boyfriend I have a constant pool of people I can go to for the harsh truth. I've always been a self-aware person; but for me, my struggle has always been knowing how to change things.

Healing the Hurt

I feel that I've grown and changed so much, which I've learned to celebrate, but I also have so much more growing to do, which excites me. I sometimes see overly angry women and I can't help but chuckle because that used to be me. But on the flip side I know I still have growth and healing to do over the issues of my past. Throughout the 23 years of my life I've experienced quite a bit of pain, mostly stemming from my relationship with my father. To the extent that a lot of my relationship issues almost parallel issues with my father. Throughout life I felt emotionally abandoned by him and that in turn has become my biggest fear in my dating life and friendships.

"Happiness is when what you think, say, and do are in complete harmony." When you think about it, that makes perfect sense. Your thoughts influence your words and actions...and the hardest part for me is controlling and changing my thoughts. Lately my biggest challenges have been just that along with learning to correct my thoughts and manage my emotions. There have been plenty of tests of my growth that I think I've been doing relatively well at. It's been nice to get true confirmation of my growth and development.

When I think about how long I lived without knowing my true worth, it's sad. But I can't dwell on the past; all I can do at this point is improve my future. I'm so proud of the person I'm starting to become and to look back on my growth is a beautiful thing. Being self-aware has always been good for me, but I'm finally able to improve upon my flaws. Getting to know myself has been beneficial in pretty much every aspect of my life.

My challenge this week from therapy is to think about the different areas in life where my lack of self-esteem has impacted my decisions. I think the biggest area impacted is my dating life. I would cling to anyone willing to show me attention, fall for that person quickly, and give that person my all hoping they'd want to marry me. Honestly, my fear of abandonment is probably what's prompting my short attention span with dating. Typically I'll start dating someone, develop feelings quickly, and my interest fades within about 2 weeks. If I'm being honest, that's me wanting to leave them before they leave me, that way I'm in control of the exit.

Sexually, my lack of self-worth has been a huge factor, especially when I was in college! I had such a need to be wanted that I settled for any attention, even if it was just in a sexual manner. I wanted to feel loved, desired, and valued so badly that I was willing to accept purely sexual relationships. The good news is that I've learned to love, desire, and value myself. And because it's starting internally, I can begin to enjoy sex without there being ulterior motives. Also it doesn't leave any huge voids when they leave for the night.

Another area impacted by lack of self-esteem has been my professional goals and aspirations. After attending a great school and completing my degree I decide to pursue a career in retail. In retrospect it was a fear of not being good enough to work in my field that allowed me to convince myself I enjoy retail. When I finally decided to go back and start grad school I took the easiest route possible. I didn't want to take the GRE or get rejected because of my grades...yet again my fear of not being good enough.

My fear of abandonment has played an impact on my friendships throughout my life. A lot of my friendships have ended in large part because of me. I often put my all into key friendships with the expectation that they'll do the same. But when they don't, which I now see as normal, my fear of abandonment leads me to push them away.

I'm not sure if my financial struggles have anything to do with my lack of self-worth. I tend to know the right thing to do financially but I tend to make the wrong decisions. I wish I knew why I'm financially irresponsible, but I'm trying to change my ways. Maybe it's because I self-sabotage and find it difficult to believe I deserve living a life of financial freedom?

A Whole New World

Things have been starting to fall in place for me and because of that I'm really peaceful. Even though things aren't in order yet, I am beginning to see the light at the end of the tunnel, and that gives me the peace I've wanted for years now. After months of feeling uneasy about my future, I guess it's nice to know things will be working out soon. My deepest prayer is that by the time my birthday comes around I feel very content in my life.

For me, feeling content in my life will look like me getting settled into my new home, feeling accomplished professionally, and being in a happy and healthy relationship. Feeling in control of my finances would ultimately be an added bonus. I'm just ready to be an adult instead of an almost adult or a legal minor.

I find myself constantly debating between my desires for a family and wanting to enjoy the freedoms of my 20s. My heart wants the unconditional love of a husband and kids, but my mind keeps convincing me to wait and enjoy life to the fullest. The issue with convincing myself to wait is the realization that I've had to do this for years already. It's very heartbreaking for me to know that I constantly have to tell myself not to want the one true desire of my heart. While I can appreciate that I now have other goals and aspirations to focus on, it doesn't remove the desires of a family from my heart. It is my hope that keeping myself busy will give me a much-needed distraction. Maybe marriage and kids will come as a surprise to me...while I'm busy with life.

Wow! It's been almost 20 days since I've written in this book! The crazy part is that's actually a good thing, because I've just been extremely busy and productive. I will however make this book more of a priority. The last month or so I have been very driven and focused on my future and the steps necessary to get there. I've been working literally around the clock in order to prepare myself for the lifestyle I want. It's a huge sacrifice and that doesn't leave much time, but I have complete confidence it will all be worth it.

My goals and aspirations have only gotten bigger and better over time! I thank God for allowing me to have such a large vision for my life at 23 years of age. The funny part is that a year ago, being a mother and wife was all I aspired to be. Taking the time to get to know myself, learn what I like to do, and create additional goals for myself has been amazing and it's probably the best thing that's happened to me! Had I gotten married when I wanted, I wonder what would now be my goals in life?

I now have goals and dreams that don't require someone else, which is healthy! They do not replace my desire for a family, however they give me something productive to focus my energy on until the time is right for me to have a family. Honestly, I see now that taking this time to focus on me is going to make me a great mother and wife. I've also learned that being selfish now will give me the ability to be completely selfless for my family. And when that time comes, I will be able to choose to be selfless without any regrets or "what ifs" or "I wish I hads". What better comfort to have? Additionally, I'm ensuring that I'm in a financial position to take care of my children's wants and needs!

Lifestyle Diet

Lately I've been really down about my current life situation, and I decided to create a lifestyle diet. I'm not sure if that's a real thing, but that's what I'm going with. For the month of June I have a list of things I will and will not do in an effort to purge and cleanse my life in every area. I plan to watch my home church online every Sunday service and bible study. It is my goal to do some form of workout EVERY

SINGLE DAY! I'm not eating any junk food with one outing allowed per week max. No outgoing communication, except to my mother of course. Also, I'm going to write daily and read at least weekly. Oh and I forgot to mention no social media postings.

By the end of June my finances, emotional state, dating life, spiritual walk, and physical health should be completely transformed. I'm not sure how God plans to turn things around for me in my life, but I'm declaring this...by the end of June, if not sooner, God will have turned things around for me. By the time July hits, I will be back to a place where I can truly enjoy life.

I don't think you're supposed to set time frames on God, but I believe in him for a breakthrough. I don't know when, where, or how...but God! I do not feel he will abandon my needs or even my desires, and I'm very sure that everything I've been going through will serve to be for my benefit. Right now I have about an hour before going to work and I've truly enjoyed taking this time for myself. I've done some relaxing and a lot of reflection, which is helpful.

I'm interested to see what will happen when I stop posting to social media and no longer make outgoing communication. How many "friends" will actually reach out to me? Who will show they care about what's going on in my life? Who's going to be there for me? What I'm even more interested to see is my physical transformation at the end of this lifestyle diet. If I'm working out daily and eliminating junk food, how amazing will my body look? I think my mother wanted to make a trip to the beach in July; my body will look kick ass by then!

The area of my finances is completely in God's hands. I'm doing everything I can to improve my situation; the rest is up to God. And I believe in him to fix it. It is my dream to live a happy and healthy life where I have the time and financial means to do everything my heart desires. I want to be able to enjoy my 20s to the absolute fullest instead of suffer through them. Who knew when I sat down to write this book for the 23rd year of my life, I'd be going through one of the biggest transitional periods ever?

This " lifestyle diet" includes no social media posting and no outgoing communication. I think I will start to see who truly cares for me, and who are my true friends. Eliminating social media posting and outgoing communication will require those who care to reach out to me. This lack of true and genuine friendships has been a tough area for me lately.

Maybe one day I'll know what it feels like to have true and genuine friends. Until then, I will continue to focus on my personal growth and development. When it's meant to happen it will, and in the meantime I will nurture the few friends I do have. My professional life has not progressed as much as I thought it would have by now. I sit here wondering what I'm supposed to be doing in life and what's the right direction for me to be going.

So, not even halfway into the month and I've failed my "lifestyle diet" in pretty much every way. I think the issue might be I tried to take on too many challenges at once. Although I've been successful at some, especially working out, I've yet to stick to any of them. Maybe going forward I can make one challenge at a time and build on from there. That may be something to consider for the second half of the year. It's hard to believe the year is almost half way over; 2015 has not at all been the year I expected it to be.

It is my deepest prayer that the rest of this year will be less stressful and that I can actually enjoy life. Between constant arguments with my ex, stress at my job followed by having no job but paying my bills on my own, the constant realization of one sided friendships, the draining inability to have the things I want, the lackluster dating life, and my weight going up and down...the past 12+ months have been draining. It is my prayer that I experience a complete turn around in my life, such that I'm able to truly enjoy being young. Since I'm not married and don't have kids, now should be the time I'm enjoying every bit of life. Yet somehow I'm not.

Transitions

Every transition has been a growth process preparing me for the next phase of my life. As with most transitional periods, it has been full of growing pains. However, what doesn't kill you makes you stronger. To me that statement means the things you go through can only build your endurance, stamina, and perseverance. I'm able to deal with tomorrow's problems because of what I'm dealing with today. Perseverance is a strong part of my character and considering I'm a very determined person, I should be soaring through life's challenges. When I make up my mind to do something, it might as well be considered done. So at this point I'm committing to getting through these struggles of life with pride.

The pride comes in knowing there is a purpose and benefit to these challenges I'm facing, having a strong belief in the God that has loved and protected me for my entire life, and finally having an understanding of myself and knowing that I'm capable of doing any and everything my heart desires. Not only do I have the ability and the grace of God, but also I have the determination to see it through.

At the end of the day, I may come home to an empty apartment and lay in my bed alone, but that's not my end result. I may be in financial shambles currently, but I won't always be here. I may have a lot of one-sided friendships, but God is preparing my heart to embrace genuine relationships. Maybe when my life seems to be going as planned I will write another book. Maybe I won't feel the need to. Maybe there will never be a point where I feel I have my life "together". I guess only time will tell, but having the ability to express myself openly about the challenges of life has been a beautiful thing.

My biggest challenge currently is learning not to give discounts to people who don't deserve any discounts. When you know your value, you'll stop giving out discounts. For me, that is my next growth assignment. I have a history of giving an underserving person a significantly discounted me. And if they still don't budge, I offer the benefits of being in my life for free. That refers to the benefits of my friendship, dating me, and of me caring. From here on out the benefits of me come at a high cost and I will no longer offer discounts when I think people can't afford me. I will instead wait patiently for those deserving a place in my life. I am no longer fearful that no one will be able to afford the costs of my benefits.

Having standards are only as good as the ones that are kept. And if I have requirements or non-negotiables for those in my life, then I need to stick to them knowing exactly what I bring to the table. Most importantly, I must be willing to eat alone if necessary until others understand my true value. And really, I'm not alone. I have my mother who has NEVER once left my side. I have a small support system that has my best interest at heart. I am learning to focusing on what and who I do having in my corner instead of focusing on the people I don't have in my corner. I've learned there's a difference between people in your corner and people in the crowd.

So, as I sit here not even wanting to start my day, I wonder how I'm going to be able to survive. There is no worse feeling than giving life your all and still coming up short. This year has not been the year I thought it would be and at this point I'm not sure how I can continue.

My finances have hit an all time low, and I can no longer see any light at the end of the tunnel. I couldn't even sleep at certain points last night because I was so sad. I feel like a complete failure and that's what hurts the most. I have made genuine efforts to be financially responsible, and yet here I am, completely unable to pay my bills. How is it possible to work two jobs and still be flat broke? Living a step below paycheck-to-paycheck, whatever that step is, that's where I've been for a while.

I've gotten really good about pretending to be happy. I've been doing that since I was a kid. I can carry a happy demeanor, but when I sit back and think...I'm not happy at all. But the true question becomes what now do I do about it? Where do I go to find true happiness? Really I just want to feel loved by someone other than my mother. I want genuine mutually beneficial friends. Is that really too much to ask? Yet I've been asking all my life. I just want a happy and healthy relationship that's working towards a family. I just want to be experiencing everything life has to offer.

I know eventually I will have all of those things, but really I'm tired of always having to wait for what I want. I feel like I'm working my life away. I just sit back and wonder will it ever be worth it and will my life ever have true meaning to it? What is my purpose in life? It gets draining feeling like you're simply floating through life with no true direction. I feel like I'm running fast but going nowhere. I just really and truly need a breakthrough in my life because I refuse to continue to live life unhappy. It's unfair to me.

My goals, my dreams, my aspirations, my focuses, and where I apply my energy have all shifted. It's crazy to think how much I've changed and grown, and the year isn't even over.

23 ...and Finally Loving Me

I can only imagine what my life will look like knowing that I'm actively growing and started at 23. What will 25, 30, 40, or 65 look like? Especially when some people never ACTIVELY grow up. So, since I'm actually trying I wonder how then will life look? I'm excited to look forward to the day where I can look back on life and smile.

Honestly, I cannot wait until I'm able to achieve my current goals, even through I'm sure they'll continue to grow. Now that I've learned what I want in life, I'm determined to achieve each of them. I'm also ensuring I'm working out daily and I've removed social media from my phone and minimizing outgoing communication. This will give me time to get myself in order and will serve as an effective refresh for my life.

Things with my sorority have been going very well, and with finishing up my first full year in this chapter it's been a beautiful thing. I've had the honor of taking on more responsibility and it has allowed me to grow within the organization. I love my sorority and being a part of such a productive chapter is a huge blessing. I genuinely cannot wait to continue to grow with this chapter! And it's helping me to grow into a better person as well, which is a win-win.

I have also been starting my days with running a mile and it has helped physically. Even though the scale has not been my friend, the mirror has been! I love the changes on the inside and outside. Now my challenge becomes sticking with it and remaining consistent, even when I don't particularly want to go for a run or exercise in general.

The past week and until the end of the month I'm taking a hiatus from social media. It has been a refreshing and surprisingly needed break from everyone else's life. It has allowed me to focus on my own life and focus on what I need to be doing. This has been very difficult to stick to, but I have! And I'm almost done!! The biggest issue has been when I'm bored.

I'm feeling much more at peace about my friends. I may not ever have mutually beneficial friends. Maybe I will. But I'm finally finding peace with either side of that coin. There are some people who I can consider genuine friends, and that is what I'm choosing to focus on.

23 ...and Finally Loving Me

I feel so confused in life and I'm at a point that I'm not sure what direction I'm supposed to be going. Sometimes I feel like I'm on a hamster wheel going full speed ahead...going absolutely nowhere. Truthfully one of my fears is unproductivity. I'm trying to figure out my life's path and understanding what steps I should be taking to improve my future. The scary part is that I have no clue at all. I'm learning to fully trust God to order my steps. The toughest part about my current life situation is feeling so isolated. Feeling like I'm in this game of life alone is a very crappy feeling. Part of me feels stupid for allowing relationships to play such an important role in my life. But isn't that normal?

Humans weren't designed to live in isolation. And it's not like I don't have access to people, I just feel that I'm lacking genuine and close companionship. And having a true relationship is always something I've wanted. It seems unfair that the things I want most seem to evade me constantly. The cruel part is that there have been several moments where I felt close to having what I want just to have the rug pulled from under me. All I want more than anything is to get it right with someone who is just as tired of getting it wrong. I try to remain patient, but it gets really tough, especially when I start to think "well maybe this is it" and it fails miserably.

Last night I had a few crazy dreams and in looking up the meanings of the different aspects a few things stuck out to me. One was a confirmation of my need to wash away the past and close those chapters, also my constant struggle learning how to ask for help, my going through a significant change/transitional phase of life, and finally the ending of a former way of thinking.

Every piece of my two consecutive dreams addressed concerns of my heart. My biggest current issue has been trying to know the direction I should be going, as a lot of different areas of life are currently sitting at a fork in the road. The tough part is trying to follow God's instruction but not quite knowing what those instructions are. It is my prayer that God makes it abundantly clear what my next steps should be. I respect that I'm currently in a preparation phase of life and that He's getting me ready for my true desires. And when I do have a happy marriage, healthy children, and a successful/impactful career...it'll all be worth it.

23 ...and Finally Loving Me

My struggle becomes that I know I should be making steps towards my future, but in what direction? I have asked God for clear direction and instruction, and I am going to trust Him to do so. Learning to ask God for what I need and trusting in Him to provide is going to be key for my growth. Knowing that my heart finally seeks to follow His direction, I know He will provide and until the direction is abundantly clear, I will make no major changes.

I recently committed to decide to leave the past in the past, including the one ex I couldn't let go of. How can I embrace the new life experiences of my future if I don't first close the door on my past? I keep wanting to meet my future husband...while still having an emotional connection to my past. It's highly contradictory.

Anyone who's ever tried to change his or her thought process is aware that is no easy task, but it is such a critical piece of growth. "So a man thinks, so is he" which means to me that whatever I think of myself is what I will become. Therefore I have to make a complete paradigm shift to reach the growth I seek to reach in all areas of life. And I am very confident that I am able to make the necessary mental adjustments.

Not only that, but the growth potential is well within my grasps as I continue to become a better me.

I feel that I'm making improvements towards learning how to ask for help when needed. But I don't think it would be fair to say that is something I've mastered. I pray that in time I will be able to ask for the help I need prior to it being a last resort. I have also been making great strides in my spiritual development. I have been watching online sermons every morning from my church back home. Not only has it been a great start to my day, but also these messages have been challenging me to improve in difficult areas.

Lately, I'd allowed myself to get frustrated feeling like my life was stuck in a transition period. I was getting angry because things weren't happening quickly enough. Reading through my journals helped me to remember that I'd asked for it! On my birthday last year I sat down and proclaimed that this year was going to be one of growth, and focusing on my growth is going to create a transition period. I haven't even reached the end of my birth year and I've been frustrated for months now. And even if my transitional period goes beyond my birthday my spiritual maturity should be able to handle that. Beyond my friendships there have been areas of life serving as consistent frustrations including my finances, dating life, my weight, career path, feeling alone, and lack of spiritual growth.

Spiritually I've been getting a lot better since finding a system that works for me. Since beginning my lifestyle diet I've been watching an online service every morning and making an effort to apply the lessons learned. Additionally, I've been paying my tithes faithfully! Taking these steps toward God allows me to feel closer to Him and be able to hear his word for my life more clearly.

My finances have been a very consistent struggle for me. But that really depends on my outlook. I went from having no income for 5 months, to getting weekly paychecks. Although things have still been tight financially, I have been able to provide for myself. I left working for the bank 10 months ago and still have managed to keep a roof over my head, my car paid, the tank full, and I haven't starved not once. That's the perspective I'm choosing to focus on.

My dating life has been a large part of my frustration. Always has been. But in reading through my journals I see now that is likely because of my inconsistency. For example, I'll say and commit to doing things one way and cave the moment I meet someone. I'll say I'm worth more but continuously give out discounts. Then I have the nerve to get frustrated about getting the same result...well what has changed?

The past few months I've gotten better about knowing my worth and refusing to accept less. Better being the key word. I've learned the difference between a guy I'm interested in and someone who may actually be right for me. I've also learned how to walk away when a situation is not right. My area of struggle seems to be learning to keep my legs closed. But even in that area I've seen progress. I no longer allow my vagina to be an entry point to my heart, instead allowing my mind (and my stomach) to be the way to my heart. At the end of the day I'm trying not to be hard on myself realizing a lot of these lesson girls were taught 10-15 years ago. I'm doing my best to learn my worth, love and respect myself, and uphold standards and expectations.

Over the past year my weight has gone up and down. But instead of realizing that my commitment to the gym has been inconsistent, I chose to focus on the lack of results. I think part of the problem has been creating these extreme goals that are a lot for me to commit to, then I get burnt out. It is my hope that with me creating realistic goals for myself I'm able to stick to them long-term. Over time I can reevaluate and improve those goals.

My career path frustrations are mildly entertaining to me. I know very clearly what I want to do in the long term, my confusion has come in with not knowing which direction to take now. What is the best thing I can do now to prepare for the future career path I want? And although that's been a frustration now, I do believe it's been made clear to me what I need to be doing.

Feeling alone. Boy oh boy! It's one of the worse feelings in the world honestly. And I have been trying to deal with this feeling. Although it's gotten better over time, every once in a while it'll come back around. The unfortunate part is that I do not know how to fix the issue. This issue remains a work in progress for me.

I want to end this entry by discussing the things that are going well for me. I have a few really solid friends I can depend on. I have the potential to earn a job that will rectify my financial struggles. I am working towards my first business venture. I am learning to enjoy the single life. I have an amazing support system. I've been able to provide for myself, despite my finances being tight. I have everything I need and more! Most importantly: I LOVE WHO I'M BECOMING!

Frustrations

Things have been very frustrating lately and I've been feeling very confused in life in general. It's been weeks since I've written, months since I worked out, and a very long time since I felt my life was together. Not knowing what to do professionally has been a huge piece of my frustrations. I hate feeling so lost all the time and not knowing what direction I should be working towards. Feeling like I don't hear from God gets frustrating, and is likely why I haven't been watching church consistently lately. I feel like nothing's changing.

23 ...and Finally Loving Me

A downside to my realization of how inconsistent I've been through reading my journals has been my lack of desire to start. It's almost as if, "since I can't stick with it why bother?" Maybe eventually I'll be able to get myself together, but I really and truly don't know how. I try to write, I try to pray, I try to seek feedback and guidance...but I always end up in the same frustrating place. When will I ever know what it feels like to truly be happy? And why must I wait so long to experience it? I feel like everything I want in life, I have to wait years and years for...and it's not fair!

How is it that ugly women get married and have babies all the time? Yet here I am an attractive young lady with a lot going for herself and can't get a guy to stick around for more than 2-3 weeks. Clearly it must be my personality, but what is it about me that is so awful? And why is it that I repel the one thing I want most in life...a family! Yet everyone around me gets to have one. I just don't understand.

This year has not at all been what I thought it would be. I thought I would be flourishing in every area of life. Professionally, financially, emotionally, spiritually, physically, and with my friendships...and yet here we are. The quote that sticks out in my heart most often is "Everything you are going through is preparing you for everything you asked for." And I truly want to believe that, but it's times like this when it seems too hard. Feels like I'm being foolish by wanting to believe in better days coming.

At the end of the day, I just want to feel joy in a real way and my heart does not feel that right about now. Honestly I don't even know if I ever felt that way or if it's even possible with my life. I haven't been able to go to therapy much lately because I just can't afford it. That breaks my heart, knowing there is help out there but I'm too broke to access it regularly. I'm reaching a place where I'm just over feeling anything. I feel myself returning to a very numb place, and I know that feeling numb for me is only a few steps away from severe depression. And that's what scares me.

Love

Freedom of Choice

Choices! I think this is the most critical part to truly enjoying life! Having the ability to choose among several different options, and then selecting the option that makes you happiest is key! Even when it comes to relationships! Actually the freedom of choice is most important when it comes to a serious committed relationship. Crazy right? But if you truly breakdown the concept of having a choice...it really makes sense.

For years every one thought the reason Will and Jada Smith have such a good celebrity marriage was because they had an open relationship. Jada recently made a statement after many years to clarify saying their relationship is not open. Instead they as adults gave each other freedom of choice and time and time again they choose to love each other! What a powerful statement to make to your partner!

To feel like you have a right to choose to be with anyone in the world, but you WANT to be with that person. I think a lot of unhappy couples are born out of feeling locked into a particular option, and that option begins to loose its appeal. Having this freedom to choose who, what, or where you feel happiest...that's where enjoying life begins. Seeking freedom in your career, friendships, partners, and community involvement is key.

A conversation with my mom lead to a revelation in my dating life. I tend to latch on to people romantically and we all know men hate that. This new information will surely be applied. I've realized that I simply have to date differently to get what I want out of my dating life. For starters, I cannot have sex with any guy I'm interested in, which honestly is difficult because it seems like such an oxymoron. But from here on out, without a commitment, I will not have sex with someone I'm dating. Sex causes problems and blurred vision on my part! And I think I've learned the hard way that unless they've worked hard for it, they won't appreciate it.

Additionally, I need to stop initiating conversations, dates, sex, all that! I also need to completely eliminate the "Netflix and Chill" moments as well. I, at some point, have to learn how to date smarter and that point is now! Insanity is doing the same thing expecting a different result! I think I am also going to order Steve Harvey's books on dating. I previously read Phaedra's book on being a southern bell...but it might be time for a reread. For the first time in my life I am starting to have a desire to read, especially if it can help me become a better woman.

One piece of advice from my mom during our powerful talk the other night (that she probably thinks I ignored) was to look into powerful women and study successful wives and mothers. This is such a radically appropriate suggestion for me and as I do my "research" I will be sure to share. As of now my goal is to look into Dominique Haddon, Myesha Chaney, Kandi Burruss, Beyonce, Phaedra Parks, and probably more.

The Struggles

I am finally starting to understand why women sometimes end up being super career focused. When you apply efforts towards your career there are concrete and very calculated results, and you can depend on those results coming at some point. Whereas, when it comes to dating there are so many unknown variables, which may or may not lead to your desired results. But why is that? Because in order to achieve the desired dating results it directly involves another person. That person has to also want the same results, apply the same effort, and have the same level of commitment. To find that person, you need luck.

You literally have to kiss several frogs, some of them are poisonous, to find your prince. And even then you might find he's really not your prince. If you're anything like me, you're a hopeless romantic finding (and blinded by) the potential in every dating prospect. This is a damaging process for me because more often than not someone undeserving is allowed into my heart, which leads to the critical debate I'm currently facing. Do I choose Person A, who is perfect on paper, religious, family oriented, motivated, and wants the same things I want? Or do I choose Person B, who isn't looking for the same long-term goals but satisfies my shallow subconscious.

Most people reading this would say Person A obviously, but Person A isn't perfect...but the effort to be better is there. But what if I wake up 10 years later feeling unfulfilled and feeling like I'm missing something in my life? In today's world that's such an easy problem to solve, you simply get a divorce. But for me marriage is a once in a lifetime opportunity and I will not enter marriage just to end up divorced. Not to mention the impact it'll have on our future children. It's just not fair. Children do not ask to be brought into the world and when their parents have issues, the children often suffer the most. Nothing bothers me more than when parents use their children as pawns, whether single parents or divorced. Withholding your child from their parent because you're upset at the other parent only hurts the child more.

I saw a quote that I wished I'd saved, but basically it referenced how the man you want and the man you need may not be the same person. Really it brings up a valid point because choosing the man you want may lead to a painful yet fulfilling life. But if you have someone ready, willing, and able to give you the deepest desires of your heart...why shouldn't you want them? Often times I let the shallow desires of my heart (good looks, great sex, and a nice body) interfere with my mind's urge to protect my heart. And although the safer option may also bring pain, is love really ever a logical decision? I find myself making a choice between what I need and the hope of finding what I want.

The New Side Chick

I read this article on social media about the new side chick. The article brought up a very interesting perspective about women who fall for a guy who's openly stated they're not ready for a relationship. Then when the guy's ready for a relationship, they meet and commit to some new girl pushing the one who stayed aside. I can be humble enough to say that I've been this version of a side chick numerous times, including in my current situationship. Waiting around for him to be ready, while giving my time, heart, and body hoping one day he'll come around. But I've always tried to operate under the principle of "if you knew better you'd do better" which isn't always so easy.

How can you walk away from someone you really like all because he's not ready? But how can you stick around knowing this situationship ends in pain? After reading the article, I felt compelled in my heart to walk away if he was unwilling to commit. The reality is I deserve commitment; any man I am dealing with should WANT to make me unavailable to others. Now this all sounds great on paper but the question then becomes application in real life. Maybe at some point I will get this dating thing right.

It's crazy to me because I'm not ready for a serious relationship like getting married, which is why I felt comfortable accepting the situationship. But now I feel like I deserve commitment even though I don't want it to be serious right now...it feels crazy. I truly believed this situationship was perfect for where I am in my life, but I now have these emotions invested. I have given him my heart by complete accident and it was not reciprocated. Talk about a dangerous place to be. I cried over a man who can go days without communication. No thanks! Never again!

What Am I Doing Wrong?

Dating karma. I often wonder if that is a real thing because if so mine is really bad. I don't know what I did in my past life, but I am certainly paying for it now. I meet, and fall for, a constant string of guys who just aren't any good for me. Even when I'm behaving appropriately, all guys seem to want is sex. I've decided to take a 30-day dating fast. And even just a few days in I've learned how crappy the potential interest I have in my life are. It is my prayer that when this fast is over God will bring the right guy into my life, because honestly, I'm sick of dating the wrong guys.

My hope is that this dating fast will give me a refresh and some time to focus on me. Since my break up with my ex, I have been consistently looking and hoping to meet the right guy for me, and at this point I'm just over it. I'm actually taking this time to do all the fun things I've always wanted to do. I'm going to the movies more often, learning new recipes, and maybe even taking a pole fitness class. I wonder what else I can add to that list of things for me to do. Being on a break from school and work, I've had a lot of time to be with myself. That time has allowed me to explore my likes/dislikes and get to know myself better. I just hope all the growth I think I'm experiencing will be worth it one day.

My dating life has been subpar with the guys I've met so far only being interested in sex. I understand sex is great, but why does that have to be the extent of it? Why is any type of commitment too much to ask? It honestly gets to be extremely frustrating to say the least. I just have to remain faithful in God that at some point the right guy will indeed come my way. And until he does I will continue to better myself and assume he's probably doing the same.

Another topic on my mind the last few days is whether it is possible to be friends after a relationship? I feel that although it is possible, it's rare and very complicated. I have only one ex that I'm actually good friends with, although I'm on good terms with all of my exes. However, my most recent ex is insisting on being friends and it's truly uncomfortable for me. Maybe it's because things are so fresh and maybe we'll never be able to have a true friendship. I think we need space but he's insisting on being a part of my life. At the end of the day, if I have to choose between him and myself then I choose me every time!

I'm not sure how I managed to end up with a true friendship with one ex, but at the end of the day I very much appreciate having him as a go-to person. Because he knows me so well, probably better than anyone, I often turn to him for sound feedback when I'm working through things. And it's reciprocated, usually when he needs advice from a female perspective about his relationship. I think because we've been done for some years now and we've both moved on, we're now able to be friends. Having someone who truly understands me at my core is very much appreciated. Sometimes it can get complicated, but at the end of the day it works for us.

One thing I've learned is that finding a good friend is very difficult lately and I've been dealing with the loss of someone who I thought was a good friend. But when a person cannot balance being a consistent friend while in a relationship, it's time to let them go. And with that friend getting married, it's pretty much official that our friendship is over. All in all I'm okay with that. I know she wants to be a wife and she truly loves him, so I'm happy for her! I'm not cutting her off but I will no longer be the only one making consistent effort towards a friendship.

Although I don't have that one close friend right now, I have a lot of people I'm cool with, and I'm learning maybe that's a good thing for me to have plenty of people to reach out to and spend time with. Eventually I will get close with someone and it'll happen naturally. I'm learning to appreciate alone time and balance that with organically developing relationships as they enter my life.

How Do You Know?

How do you know when someone is right for you? Is there some secret formula that will tell you if they're "The One"? Is it a gradual feeling or does it hit you right away? Is love at first sight a real possibility? Now "first sight" might be a connection fueled by lust, but I think the idea of knowing early on is a real possibility. For example, when you're getting to know a person on a deep level and everything you learn furthers that interest and most importantly there's a natural connection in pretty much every area.

When you feel like they're not only a good person, but the right person as well...there will be no greater feeling. But as these feelings of infatuation arise I feel the need to suppress them and conceal the true depth of my feelings, and I feel that if I allow myself to experience these feelings I might be setting myself up for heartbreak. Sometimes I wish I could fast forward a little to see how things end up, just to know everything in life will be okay or just to prepare myself for otherwise.

In addition to someone being a true gentleman, having the ability to mentally stimulate me is the biggest turn on. Having such a natural connection and feeling that person understands or "gets you" . . . well, there is truly no greater feeling. I guess only time will tell where things will take me. But since breaking up with my ex, this is the first time I'm hopeful things will feel right.

When it comes to dating, I typically meet a guy and loose interest within 2-3 weeks. But since getting to know myself better, I've also learned what I want in a partner. I've come to realize what I'm not willing to entertain, allowing me to determine my interest level quickly. I'm currently hoping to learn how to balance that better. I get really into a potential and then I drop interest completely, sometimes without notice. I need to learn how to better manage the intensity and speed I develop feelings as well as lose interest. Easy come, easy go! The problem is I want to be with someone on a long-term basis, but the easy come, easy go methods aren't going to get me to happily ever after. Maybe I'm not as ready for a relationship as I think. Maybe I'm confusing my wants with being ready for a relationship. Only time will tell.

This time of year is always filled with commercialized love. It makes me question the validity of it all. If Valentine's Day (or birthdays and anniversaries) is the only time of the year you find it necessary to make your partner feel special, there are deeper problems in the relationship. Additionally, why is the sole focus of this holiday women? Why can't women do something special for the men in their lives? In moments like this I have a special appreciation for same sex couples, because it requires effort from both parties!

I understand men and women need and give differently in their relationships. But both parties should be willing to give more effort than they require. I challenge the though that relationships require a 50/50 mindset...there should be a 100/100 balance. I give you my all and you give me your all...and we're both taken care of. Maybe one day I will meet someone who can help me test this theory. With a relationship like that, it may end up as my last relationship, which wouldn't be a problem with me!

Lately my dating life has been going pretty well, and certainly a challenge of my emotional development and growth. The guy I've been seeing lately has proven to me that breaking things off with my ex was the right thing for me. The connection I have with him is genuine, natural, and pretty much amazing. We have such a great connection on every level. I now know that what I was looking for is at least possible. He wants to take things slow and work on being friends first, which is usually where my emotional tests come in. But he's already survived my short attention span, so I'm thinking he may be around for a while.

Learning to manage my emotions has been challenging, but passing the tests have been worth it. Managing my outgoing communication and trying to balance out my developing feelings for him have been my biggest tests. In the meantime, I've been enjoying getting to know this guy. He's a good guy who's also right for me. Most importantly he challenges me to be better in a way that only one other person has before.

Now I can appreciate intimacy on a whole new level and allow myself to experience all parts of a relationship. Although I really enjoy sex, I end up craving so much more from a partner. I want a connection on every level and I find a mental connection to be the most important piece. Feeling like you're kindred spirits with someone is the best feeling in the world.

Lately it's been nice to have someone who feels like a really good friend that you connect well with. There's this natural mix between feeling so comfortable with someone, but getting so nervous around them, and feeling like you just can't get enough of them. My biggest challenge in dating him so far has been leaning to manage the pace of my developing feelings for him. It becomes increasingly difficult because since I've gotten to know myself and what I need in a partner, I now can identify when I've met the right person, and when things feel so right. But learning to slow down my heart and simply enjoying the moment is my true test of growth.

Why Not Me?

Unfortunately things did not work out with him, and we decided to part ways. I've been slightly down about my lack of a relationship, even to the point I've broken into tears. Part of me ends up missing my ex, but I think in actuality it's me missing having someone in that role. I have a lot coming onto my plate that will keep me busy and I'm hoping it'll distract me. Having a busy schedule will require me to focus on bettering myself and accomplishing my goals.

What's crazy to me is that with all that I have going for myself, there is still the void of companionship. I try not to focus on this void, but sometimes it randomly hits me. I was driving and listening to music and broke into tears despite seemingly being in a good mood. All in all things are starting to work themselves out. Every area of life is BEGINNING to piece together, and I can finally see the light at the end of the tunnel. I feel confident to say within the next few months things will be worked out! That gives me peace.

It really would be nice to have someone to call my own and share life with, but until then I will have to continue to focus on my growth. I thought I was getting close to having someone special in my corner, but it turns out that's not the case. Now I sit and wonder if and when "the one" will walk into my life and refuse to walk out of it. That's what I'm waiting for! Until then I am focused on being the woman my future husband deserves.

If You Knew Better...You'd Do Better

My current dating growth exercise is learning to be more of a challenge. I get hit on all the time, but there hasn't been much quality and it may be partly my fault. According to my ex, a guy's behavior is largely dependent on mine. Even something as simple as getting my phone number is a privilege that needs to be earned. Additionally, communication should be incoming only. One thing I need to stop allowing is home visits because it's a dating gateway drug. Eliminating home visits may be my biggest chance of eliminating premature sexual encounters. I wish I knew how to tell myself no, but when I'm interested in someone it's tough to stop sex from happening.

My therapist believes that I use sex to regain my power, particularly after a breakup. When my ex from college and I broke up I was devastated and lashed out sexually seemingly in an attempt to regain power and control of my dating life. With my recent ex, after our first break up I was still hurt and became slightly promiscuous, but after our final break up I was emotionally done and had minimal episodes of lashing out. With this information I have to learn how to manage my behaviors, expectations, and place parameters on myself, particularly after being disappointed. Clearly the dating game isn't going to change, so in order to get to the relationship I want I have to learn how to play that game efficiently. Thankfully I now have a dating coach to help see me through, because clearly on my own I'm struggling severely.

As far as my dating life is concerned, it's been pretty much non-existent lately. I'm currently in a place where I'm willing to just let it be. Whoever is meant to be in my life long-term,

God will bring them into my world. I finally feel truly ready to handle the responsibility of a relationship, because that is not an easy task to prepare for. Sometimes having that time to myself is exactly what I need to process and prepare.

It is time I make changes also in my perspective of my dating life. I'm learning that my thought process attracts the men I meet into my life. I have to learn to focus on the positive and the type of characteristics I do want in my dating potentials. I want to meet someone who is established in life, ready for commitment, and desires to work towards marriage. My thought process needs an adjustment in all areas of life as well. With regards to my emotional growth, my finances, my friends, my professional development, pretty much every area of my life needs a paradigm shift.

Dating has been a complicated adjustment, especially when being involved with someone who has an extremely busy schedule. I often find myself trying to find a balance between being understanding of someone with a busy schedule and knowing my worth. I'm hoping to be able to figure out a way to make that scenario work, because if you don't want a broke partner you have to deal with a busy one. It could potentially pay off in the long run, but only time will tell for sure. In the meantime I'm going to focus on my personal growth and allow any dating interests to show their true intentions. The toughest part of dating is learning to believe the signs that are right in front of your face.

For me, my biggest flaw is seeing only the good in people until they begin to hurt me. There could've been several warning signs to show their motives or true intentions, but I always hope for the best in people. The sad reality is I end up the one hurt because I made the choice to see the good in them. Maybe one day, hopefully soon, I will be surrounded by friends and family who truly mean well for me. It would be nice to experience emotional stability in the area of interpersonal relationships. What a beautiful feeling to have long-term connections with the people in my life.

Last night while clearing out stuff preparing to move, I came across some really old letters and poems from my ex in high school. I only got a chance to read one, but even in just that one letter it showed me exactly how much I'm missing in my dating life. He really loved me, thought the world of me, and truly felt I was The One for him. And although my feelings for him are long gone, I want that type of feeling with someone. I deserve that!

Not only do I want to receive unconditional love and total adoration from someone, I want to feel the same way about them as well. That to me is how I'll know I met The One. Until then I will continue to wait. This process of having to wait becomes increasingly frustrating for me to deal with. The most frustrating part is that every time I start to feel content, I meet someone who I think has potential and time and time again it's fool's gold. I feel like I deserve to be in a happy and healthy relationship but my friendships are lack luster too. I just don't understand. If I'm the good person I think I am, then why can't I maintain healthy connections with people?

Family

Where It All Began

Family has always been a huge part of my life, even after leaving the nest. And that's still true, in fact being there for my family brings me true happiness...so that's what I do! As my family continues to grow and expand, that just means more people for me to love! Around Christmas time, I had the chance to truly enjoy spending time with my family. I truly wish more people realized Christmas is not about buying everything in the mall, it's about spending time with family. And really Christmas is about celebrating the birth of Christ. But as with most holidays, it has become a retail cash cow.

My relationship with my mother, although not perfect, is becoming better as I've gotten older over the years. She has raised me to be a self-sufficient adult and trusting that allows her to respect me as an adult. Over time she has become like a big sister to me, someone I can turn to for advice whenever I need her, and considering her delusions involving her age, maybe big sister makes the most sense.

The crazy part is that pretty much everyone in my immediate family has some delusions around their age. Why is getting older such a problem for people? I say this as someone who is 23, but seriously is it THAT bad? My mother is not even old, especially when you compare her to most moms of people my age, but my grandmother, uncle, mother, and now even my older cousins all feel the need to make up some random age for themselves.

I think my take away will be a vow to enjoy life to the fullest and learn to experience all that life has to offer. My thoughts are they lie about their age in order to attempt to recapture those moments and enjoy life again. The irony of it all...each of them had kids young. As badly as I want children, I hope they come at a time when I'm truly ready. That I've grown up and dealt with my hurtful past, that I've enjoyed life and completed my pre-baby bucket list, and that I don't feel resentment for the years I missed out on. Maybe when I'm ready for kids I will pop out a whole clan of children, with every one planned and on purposed.

This past weekend I spent time with my family and sorority sisters. It truly brought such a feeling of joy into my heart, especially getting to catch up with my neophytes! They make me so proud! For me, family is such a critical piece of my happiness! Things may not always be great but I love them with all my heart. Family is what truly pushes me to succeed. Most of my goals and aspirations are in some way tied to someone in my family.

I truly hate being so far away from my family. It's bittersweet because I love living down south, but I miss being in close proximity to them. It's my hope that eventually they'll come down south and I can make that happen! And of course one day I hope to extend my branch of the family tree. It would be nice to create my own subgroup of my family. II truly believe that when the time is right it will happen, but the thought of my future family brings a feeling of peace to my heart.

Family is a very important part of my life, and often times I get sad that I'm so physically far from my family. Although I really enjoy being in this new city, it's further than I'm used to. I truly miss being 30 minutes – 1 hour away from my mother and sister. This week in therapy I was able to uncover (with help of course) that a part of the reason I want to be a mother is possibly because of the value my mother has in my life. Before this journey being a mother and wife was the only way I felt I could have value.

My mother and sister came to visit for mother's day, followed by my sister staying for a few weeks. Having my sister down here has forced me to slow down in life and enjoy the little things. That has been so beneficial to my mental health and me. I enjoyed spending time with her and catching up on a one-on-one basis. I can't believe how fast she's growing up and all the memories over the years! In the fall she'll be starting high school; it's so mind blowing. She makes me so proud in so many different ways!

Family Goals

For the first time in my life my goals and aspirations go far beyond being a mother and a wife. I think that shows growth and maturity. Ironically it took breaking up with my ex to learn what I truly wanted for myself. I'm so glad that I have goals for myself now because it gives me something to focus on, and I have goals that are fueled by my own efforts, not necessarily involving someone else to share my dreams or timeline.

This year I would like to experience restoration with the estranged areas of my family. I recently reconnected with my cousin who's been distant for years. And as important as family is to me, it really warmed my heart to be able to sit and speak so openly with him. It is my personal goal to be able to work on the reconciliation of my relationship with my grandmother and to be able to work past the hurt she's caused. It took years for me to move past the hurt from my father; I simply hope it doesn't take that long with my grandmother. I don't enjoy living in a place of pain.

One thing that amazes me is when some single mothers think it's possible to fill the void of their child's father. Giving your child love, fulfilling their needs, and being a constant in their life it doesn't replace the need for their father. For a girl, her father is her first example of love and is often associated with her self-esteem. For a boy, his father provides an example of what a man looks like.

Now mothers are just as important, but for different reasons. I wish more single mothers understood they cannot serve both roles. I hope our generation returns to the two-parent household, because it's truly critical. Women are special and powerful creatures but we simply cannot do it all. I hope one day women understand (again) that needing a man doesn't make you weak; men need women as well. It makes us both stronger because we bring different things to the table with good reason, because we are completely different creatures.

Daddy Issues

The Deeper Impact

While watching an episode of "Sex and the City", it brought up a valid point that I found it necessary to dissect. The question Carrie asked was "How much does a father figure, figure?" Anyone who knows me knows that I have a very strained relationship with my father, although very few know all of the details. It's commonly stated that a father-daughter relationship plays a major role in a girl's life, particularly when it comes to dating. But what do you do when your father never seemed to be able to figure it out? It's not like I can go back in time and make him do better...so now what?

So many people tell me how my ill feelings towards my father have an adverse impact on my romantic relationships, but how am I supposed to deal with it effectively so that it does not continue to impact my interpersonal relationships and continue to impact me? What is the benefit of a relationship with my father as an adult? I personally feel that 23 years later, he's had enough chances to be a man and step up in my life. At this point in life I just aim to find a man who can be a good man in my life. I need someone who will fight for me, be a consistent support in my life, and has a genuine understanding that my love cannot be bought.

Until that man comes into my life I will continue to grow and develop into a better woman, one worthy of his love. That is no easy task because I have a lot of "make up" work to do in order to learn to love myself. Sometimes I sit in tears heartbroken at the realization that I don't love myself and that I honestly don't know how. I've come to learn that it all begins with a true sense of self-worth and falling in love with yourself through getting to know yourself fully.

As strong and confident as I portray myself to be, deep down inside I'm an alone little girl wanting to be loved. This innate fear of abandonment causes problems for me and I wish that it didn't. I think the #1 reason I haven't had a child, despite my deep desire to have a baby, is because of my father. No child deserves a father going in and out of his or her life because it got too hard to love them, and because of that I choose to wait until I am able to create a family with the full partnership of a good man.

My fear, however is that I'll never experience my one true desire. When you've lived your life feeling like you're not good enough, it's hard to believe you'll actually get the desires of your heart. Maybe one day I will learn to trust that God won't abandon me or ignore the desires of my heart, but trusting God means giving Him complete control to bring those desires to my life when He feels that I'm ready.

Having my father refuse to fight for a place in my life led to me to feel like I wasn't worth it. Every time I hurt his feelings he would go MIA in my life, for months or even years at a time. When I wanted him to fight for me...he didn't. Whether that was because he didn't know how to or didn't want to, either way he didn't. My biggest challenge becomes knowing how to deal with my daddy issues so that they do not continue to impact my relationships. I've had conversations with my father but they're usually full of excuses and weak explanations. He's apologized for hurting me, but what am I supposed to need from him as an adult?

Where Do I Go From Here?

As an adult I feel that it is unnecessary to try to rebuild a relationship with my father. I don't know what it would fix. If he had died would I be stuck with the pain for the rest of my life? I refuse to believe it and no one seems to be able to explain the benefits of restoring that relationship. The question I've had for 5+ years has been around how to move past the pain this relationship, or lack thereof, with my father has caused. I think I've grown a lot from the pain as well. Several years ago even Father's Day would bring about hurt, anger, and even tears. But I've been able to move past it and learn to acknowledge the good fathers I know, and I even look forward to celebrating Father's Day with my future husband one day.

Yesterday was my father's birthday and my mother kept pressuring me to reach out to him. She kept implying that it was a symbol of my growth and that me not reaching out to him means I'm still living in pain, but that's not true! Honestly I hate when she gets on these tangents about my father because she's always pushing me to reconcile with him. I have no desire to do so, and I have made that clear to her but she insists that I'm not healed from the hurt he's caused if I don't want to reconcile. I have zero desire to start a new relationship with him, and I refuse to believe that's my only way to be healed. It's basically implying that if he'd passed away I'd be stuck with the pain for the rest of my life. As if he's the only one who can heal the hurt he's caused, but that's not the case at all.

As Father's Day approached, I debated how I was going to respond. This year apparently Hallmark has released Father's Day cards for single mothers. The worse part is they did so only in the Mahogany (African American) section. In a moment of transparency, there was once a time that I would wish my mom a happy Father's Day. I came to the realization that me doing so was me responding from a place of pain and bitterness. I have since learned that my mother could never replace my father's role in my life, regardless of how good of a mother she has been for me!

This year for Father's Day, I've decided I'm going to acknowledge those men I know who are being great dads to their children. I'm thankful to no longer have bitterness in my heart towards my father, and I've finally learned to release the pain that he's caused. All I can do is learn to restore/heal my heart. To all of the good dads out there, Happy Father's Day! This Father's Day has been a relatively good day even given the historical difficulties of the day. That to me shows growth and healing from the pain of a lackluster father. It really is an unfortunate situation that I could be so beautiful (inside and outside) and be abandoned by the one person responsible for my procreation. There was a time when I thought that abandonment was because I wasn't good enough, but the truth is that my father is not good enough to be my parent.

Healing From The Hurt

The sad truth is too many children take the lack of parental involvement personally and accept the guilt and shame as their own. That is a hard paradigm shift to make, causing one to completely alter the natural thought and it wasn't until I was working actively towards my growth that I started to make that shift. I have learned to accept Father's Day as a day to acknowledge those who are involved fathers. I wish more men would choose to step up and handle the responsibilities they helped to create.

All I can do at this point is pray that I make a wise choice for my children.

Part of my therapy session homework is focusing on the "anger" I have towards my father. I put quotes around anger because my biggest question to myself is regarding whether am I truly angry or not? Do I still harbor hate in my heart for him? I know there's a deep irritation for his decisions and the truth is I think he's a punk for not stepping up to face his responsibility as a father, but I'm pretty sure the hate or anger is gone from my heart at this point in my life.

From what I understand, my father would consistently contribute financially, which is necessary and I'm sure helped my mother to provide for me. As a child the money meant absolutely NOTHING to me. I needed him there physically and emotionally, which unfortunately some fathers don't understand. The sad part is I should've been a blessing in his life, especially as his only child, yet he wasn't mature or strong enough to handle that blessing. The unfair part for me is that him not being man enough to raise me as his daughter has left me with emotional scars I need to find a way to heal. And those scars run so deep that I'm now realizing only God can heal them from the inside out. To fully recover it will take some time, but in all honesty it has been hard to move past the pain of a relationship that has impacted me so much.

This one person is the reason for 50% of my genetic makeup. Even something as simple as my severe food allergies come from his side of the family. I look just like him, and according to my mother I make similar faces as him. There are these similarities among many other things, so how do you truly move past the pain of such a critical relationship? A girl's father is her first interaction with love and sets the tone for how she expects to be treated. It takes a long time (and is something I'm still working on) to learn not to fear abandonment. My father taught me that if I'm too difficult to deal with, it's okay to just walk away. And he did this several times; maybe he really wanted me to learn that lesson.

In dating relationships I have a tendency to push people away to see if they care enough to stick around, and if they start to leave me, my fear of abandonment pushes me to cling to that person for dear life. Actually that goes for all relationships, which is so unhealthy. I have gotten a lot better about not pushing people away and not clinging because they want to walk. I'm learning that if they can't treat me as I deserve to be treated, they aren't supposed to be in my life anyway, and being at peace with that. That's why I decided to stop speaking to my father after 20 years of him going back and forth...I don't feel he deserves to be in my life.

Honestly I've been able to heal those scars a lot since asking him to leave my life. Him going in and out of my life was picking at my emotional scars. As with all scars they cannot be healed if they're constantly being picked at. Now, I can process the impact he's had on my life and make progress towards correcting the impact of his mistakes. The more I process my emotional scars I see that he might honestly be the reason I have yet to have kids. I refuse to bring children into this world for them to suffer from the same pain caused in my heart. Later I will also be faced with the decision of whether or not to allow him into the lives of his grandchildren. Let me tell it, he doesn't deserve that privilege.

To my future children, it's my responsibility to protect you from the pain caused by inconsistency. Whether that pain is coming from your father or grandfather, it's my job to minimize that pain on your behalf. It's my deepest prayer that I can keep that promise to protect you, as my future children. Please know that I love you more than words can speak, and I vow my life to your betterment.

Friends

Learning From the Past

Friends. How many of us have them? For me having lasting and genuine friendships has always been an area of complication for me. Maybe I simply expect too much from people I consider friends, but honestly it's just the expectation of reciprocity. When I have a friend that I'm close to, I'm all in. I spend quality time with them, their birthday becomes a priority for me, and I care about the things going on in their life. Often times it baffles me when asking for the same treatment in return is asking for too much, but I guess that's how the cookie crumbles.

Most of my friendships have ended as a result of me feeling like they didn't have time for me, my birthday not being a priority, or feeling like they just never seem to understand me. My goal for this year, in addition to those previously mentioned, is to learn how to be a better friend. Repairing my interactions with friends, I truly feel starts with learning to love myself, which will put less pressure on my friends to love me.

In talking to my mother the other night, she brought up a good point for me to reflect on. When I meet someone I feel I get along with, I tend to latch onto that person, which is extremely unhealthy. I think it stems from my fear of being alone mixed with feeling like I am not good enough. After having this realization I can now make a conscious effort to correct this behavior going forward. I've always been a firm believer in the concept of "if you knew better, you'd do better". Therefore, it would be detrimental to any future friendships if I did not apply this new revelation.

Over the course of my life a lot of times things have been given to me. In a way it has created the very spoiled person that writes these words. So many times I have bragged about being spoiled as if somehow that's a good thing, but as I have continued to grow and develop, I've learned that I shouldn't be spoiled, but instead I should spoil others. For me that means instead of expecting others to reach out, why not reach out to others if I want to speak to them. Instead of feeling down about people not being invested in my life, be invested in theirs. Instead of being hurt by having one-sided friendships, why not learn to embrace it as my reality. If giving of myself makes someone else's life a little brighter, I will begin to accept that as my reciprocation.

There was once a time when I was such a nice person, and unfortunately I allowed the world to change me. I learned in middle school that people take advantage of giving people and I chose to become an angry black woman. I thought that was the only way to protect myself from being used. Because as a person I have a very sincere inability to say "no" to others, I felt that if I were naturally rude it would minimize people asking things of me. However that had an adverse effect and it took 10+ years to realize that's not how to handle things. I can't do anything to change the past; I can only grow to be a better me. Going forward I intend to embrace my natural desire to love, care, and give, but I will also learn how to balance that with my personal needs being my top priority. I will continue to learn who I am and protect myself differently, but most importantly I will learn how to say no when the cost is too high.

Over the years, there have been many times I've been accused of cutting people off easily. But for me, it really falls down to an unwillingness to tolerate unnecessary drama in my life. Why should I fight, argue, and bicker with someone I'm not even in a romantic relationship with? Friendships should not require unnecessary drama. In an attempt to protect my peace, I'm learning to fall back from toxic people in my life. I've learned how to block phone numbers of those I truly want no dealings with. At the end of the day I'm no longer willing to beg for people's time and attention, nor am I willing to fight and scrape for friendships that no longer improve my life.

Loving Me Too

I'm extremely introverted and I have learned to protect my alone time instead of allowing others to dictate when I get alone time. Also I have been learning to respect my goals and place them as my priority over the goals of others. Most importantly I have learned that my peace deserves to be protected, particularly within my home. For example, this guy asked to come over a few months back and I told him no because of the constant drama between he and I, but that same day I invited another friend over to my house because she and I have a good time together. That was my first step in learning to protect my peace.

"No" is not a word I've previously used comfortably and that has led to me giving people more of me than they may deserve. But even if it's them asking of my time, I'm learning to evaluate whether my investment is worth it. If I'm not truly interested, then I will end up resenting helping or giving of myself, when that time could've been used differently. I have to learn not to do things because I feel like I'm supposed to. Instead I plan to do things because they feel right in my heart. And when I do things for others it'll be because I truly want to; reciprocation will be a bonus instead of a requirement.

Although life is rough right now I'm okay with it because it's all part of the process. It's truly okay to be down right now because it has given me the ability to grow and develop in a way that's most beneficial. Writing been such a huge part of my development. It provides me with a much-needed release and allows me to vent in a way that doesn't provide judgments.

Instead writing allows me to self-analyze and helps me find clarity on the issues I'm facing. Through that clarity I am able to make decisions for myself on how to move forward when faced with the challenges of life.

There are few people in my life that I feel comfortable being completely open with, three actually. I'm very thankful for these three because they truly understand me at my core and that allows me to be honest and receive necessary feedback to become a better me. Regardless of the frequency of our communication, I'm very thankful to have these people in my life. I just hope I can always count on them being in my life. The common issue I have is that I often push valuable people out of my life, usually through excessively high expectations of them, but I think I'm doing better with regards to friendships.

My biggest issue is getting past things when someone has hurt me, but I've learned to just take time and space from that person to process things. When I'm ready to interact with them again it may require me to reclassify them in my life along with my expectations of their role in my life. At times, however, it may become lonely feeling like I don't have true and genuine friends. I was even told that at my age I should have so many more friends. Although I have plenty of people I consider friends, for me to consider them my best friend is deeper than that. If I am currently without that go to person, it's okay. In the meantime I'll continue to focus on my development.

Sometimes I really have to remind myself that I'm becoming a better person and that my efforts have been very productive. I get so focused on the growth I want to see in myself that I tend to ignore the growth I've already experienced. It's so difficult to see the progress where there aren't tangible results. I do feel that my outlook on life has changed drastically and my ability to enjoy life has increased.

What's Next?

I've learned to be upfront and honest with my friends and I've learned to respect their space. I now enjoy and respect my own space as well. Honestly, I really have learned to enjoy alone time instead of feeling the need to fill that alone time with anyone willing. I also realized I'm getting closer to loving myself, and because of that I can love my friends in a healthy way. I'm at a place where I truly like myself and really that's the start. I have a feeling love for myself is growing.

Throughout this year I've been on somewhat of an emotional roller coaster. My standards have improved as a reflection of my improved self-esteem, but that also eliminates the fluff conversations and space filling interactions. While I've learned to appreciate alone time, what happens when there's nothing to fill that void? I have no job right now, school is on a break, I'm not dating anyone, and I have one good friend in a new area. I find myself in this space of emptiness wondering what to fill the void with.

I've recently taken some time to stop reaching out to friends and family that I consistently have one-sided relationships with. It gets frustrating being the only person always responsible for initiating conversations and being there for everyone else. It makes me feel like very few actually care about me...except of course when they need something from me. When I need someone to be there for me, when I need a little bit of reciprocation, no one seems to be genuinely invested, particularly those I am consistently providing support for.

I try not to let it bother me much, especially considering I've been in one-sided friendships a majority of my life, but at times it becomes overwhelming to know that most of my "friendships" are fueled by my efforts and what I can do for them. My current challenge to myself is learning to give of myself without expecting anything in return, but during a time when I feel like I need true and genuine friendships and relationships...it's a tough pill to swallow. Feeling like I have my mother and one true friend, it's just not fun. It is my prayer that I am able to grow and develop healthy and two-sided friendships.

It's always sad when you come to the realization that you just have to let people go, particularly those you were once close to, but sometimes growing apart is both natural and inevitable. Learning to be okay with that is the key for my growth and development. Throughout my life I've always had few very close friends. As time goes on those friendships begin to change and life begins to pull us in different directions.

In the past it would really hurt to realize a good friendship just isn't that anymore, but now I think I'm okay with it. Part of me being okay is because I know another good friend is going to come into my life in due time. This is currently happening with my one good friend I have down south. Now that she's married, I can tell things will be different. We may never be as close as we once were...and that's okay. Her priority now is being a wife.

Lately I've been making a true effort to go out and do things more often. Whether it be doing something with my sorority sisters, joining meet up groups, or even events my apartment complex is having, I'm truly just trying to get out of the house and enjoy myself as much as possible. Being in a new area where I don't know anyone has been extremely difficult, particularly with me being such an introvert! But I am finding ways to break out of my shell in a manner that I'm comfortable with.

Lately I feel like I've been losing more and more friends, but I'm at a place where I'm okay with it. Sometimes you just have to let go of a friendship that no longer betters you. If the existence of the friendship requires more than

I'm getting back, I'm no longer interested! From now on that energy is being placed towards bettering me. I cannot continue to be a part of one-sided friendships where people continue to take from me emotionally, or my time, or even take advantage of my naturally giving heart.

I need people in my life who are going to motivate my growth, support me as much as I support them, and be an overall asset to my life. I may not have many friends and that's likely my fault, but at the end of the day I'm a good person! I know I'm not the best person and I'm very aware that I have many flaws, but I've learned my value and I know what my presence in someone's life means. I think I still have a lot of growing to do, particularly with friends.

I've come leaps and bounds with my attitude and learning to have a positive point of view. Additionally, I'm learning how to be a giving person without any expectation of reciprocity. One area that I've realized is still a problem area for me is with my interpersonal relationships. I'm a pretty accomplished person in the areas of life that I have sole control over (i.e. academics, professionally, etc) but when it comes to the areas of life involving someone else (i.e. friends, dating, and even family) I seem to be failing.

Over the year, I felt like an area of life that I've started getting better regarding is with friendships! I've learned to apply appropriate boundaries, which helps me manage my expectations. Also, learning to minimize my interactions with people who don't have my best interest in mind has proven to be key. Being that I'm a natural giver, I have learned to control my interactions with people who are takers. It's okay to be a giver, but I cannot allow myself to give so much of myself to a person who consistently refuses to give back.

Challenges of Growth

Lately I've been a little down by the lack of genuine friendships I have in my life. This past year has taught me who's truly in my corner vs. who's simply in the audience to spectate. There have been people closer in the audience that I have mistook as being in my corner, but I have now learned the difference. With that being said, I have learned to embrace a very unorthodox friendship with my ex from several years ago. Although our romantic relationship caused a great deal of pain, we've grown to a place of a very genuine friendship. He's one of very few (maybe the only) people who truly understands me and because of that I'm able to talk to him about everything and get honest, candid, and impactful advice. That to me is the most valuable friendship!

The scary part is that deep down inside some of those feelings are still there and honestly might always be. I've tried not being his friend and the feelings are practically the same, therefore I made the decision to put those feelings aside to allow us to be genuine friends. It's not always easy to manage those feelings, but the friendship we have now makes it worth it. The other night he gave me the best piece of dating advice that I plan to apply to the best of my ability. Most importantly not just what to do, but how to do them!

The biggest current trigger for my life is a lack of true and genuine friendships. I'm there for so many people without the bat of an eye, but who's genuinely invested in my life and cares about me? I can think of two, maybe three people (including my mother). This week in therapy I left with something to think about.

Why is it that I'm more comfortable with having male friends than female? Throughout life I've always had a small yet close circle, and it's always been easier for me to be friends with guys than girls. What is it that keeps me from developing deeper friendships with other women, besides my norm of having one or two friends? I've always valued having small support systems that I know are genuine, as opposed to having a larger less connected group of friends. Personally, I don't see a need to change that.

What I would like to work on is being able to develop and maintain genuine friendships with women. I think for me, my biggest piece is working on managing my expectations of other women. Typically I expect primarily reciprocity of effort, investment, and attention. If I feel that's not being met, I get really offended and eventually will cut all ties with that person. Usually when I decide to cut ties with someone that's a permanent decision for me, as I don't make that decision lightly. I'm realizing most genuine friendships I have with men have all happened naturally, which is a privilege I haven't given to women. I'm currently working on gradually and passively allowing friendships with women to develop. Slow and steady vs. easy come easy go.

I feel that I'm finally at a place of maturity to be able to handle true friendships. I respond to disappointments differently by addressing the issue calmly and completely moving on from them. Also, I'm learning to address any problems I have with someone prior to allowing the problems to harden within my heart. One of the toughest challenges I've faced so far has been teaching people how to treat me. In my opinion, that includes setting expectations, handling disappointments appropriately, and learning to truly forgive people, even if they don't deserve my forgiveness. Through this adjustment, I almost immediately noticed people beginning to take advantage of my kind heart, which was a huge pain point. So my next attempt at protecting myself was to stop being a giver. I stopped being there for everyone, stopped giving of myself, and overall being who I was at my core. Changing a core piece of yourself is not healthy by any means, and is usually short lived. I had to find a better way because I deserved better!

Finally I realized if I keep the right people around, I don't have to censor my naturally giving heart. I learned to distance myself from people who were taking advantage of me and embrace others who had similar hearts like mine. Now everyone I'm closest to has my best interest in mind, and I feel safe being who I am. Additionally, I had to learn how to fluidly readjust the categories I've placed people in. Previously, if we weren't close anymore then you were cut off for life. Now I can see that a relational dynamic can change several times throughout life, and that's okay!

Having found an effective support system in my life has been crucial to my growth. Not only do they hold me accountable and encourage me to be better, they also remind me of my progress. I have people in my corner who will alert me to the fact that I'm being too hard on myself, or to remind me to relax, or remind me that I deserve better. Those that I'm closest to truly support my goals and me! They're the people I go to (2nd to God) when I need help to make a decision. They debate the issue with me, help me to think through the potential issues, and often times confirm what I already know or think. I am really thankful for the group of friends I have and those I interact with on a regular basis. Instead of focusing on who's not a good friend, I started focusing on who is a good friend. And I'm thankful.

Friendships have been a struggle for me for most of my life, although thankfully I finally feel like I'm at a place of security with my friends. For starters, the best part is feeling like I have true friends who are more than one sided. I now have people in my corner who are there for me and support me like I do for them. I have learned to focus on the consistent support system I do have instead of those who simply take from me. Additionally, I've learned to be flexible in my category placement of the people in my life. Some people are true and genuine all the time, some are great friends when you see them regularly, and some just don't know how to be good friends at all. Learning to be okay with the different types of friendships I have has contributed to my peace regarding friendships. I have a few people in my circle who I know are true friends that I can depend on! That's what I choose to focus on.

I have been making an effort to maintain healthy connections with those I'm close to while also being open to the idea of forming new connections. Balancing healthy expectations by monitoring my investment into others has been helpful for me. I realized I was putting more into others prematurely, getting hurt by a failure of reciprocity, and lashing out from that place of pain, which created an unhealthy cycle for me. Now I try to allow relationships (friendly, romantic, and otherwise) to develop naturally. I do so by minimizing my connection to that person and making sure what I give (time, energy, etc.) is aligned with realistic expectations. I'm beginning to understand that in order to make lasting connections I must first develop healthy foundations. It's funny because I used to be proud of being shallow, but I have grown past a lot of that and begun to focus more on a person's character. I now get to know someone's value, or lack thereof, to my life in a clear manner and allow a person's actions to weigh more than their words, which is a tough one.

Career

Professional Autonomy

Professional freedom is one of my current desires, and I'm extremely passionate about it. Working a 9-5 just doesn't work for me anymore! I find myself craving professional freedom the more I learn to put myself first. I truly feel that I was destined for a different life and I want so much more. Some people are perfectly happy in Corporate America while working their way up the ladder. I passionately believe that's not who I am meant to be. My mother has had her own company for almost 15 years and watching her support two children on her own as an entrepreneur has been breathtaking! Through her I've seen a strong ability to withstand the difficulties of entrepreneurship, enjoy the luxuries of complete autonomy, and have a complete trust in God to make things work. That has been coupled with her consistent reminders that I'm not the average person...and that an average life just isn't good enough!

Lately I've been reflecting on my decision to leave my job to pursue my dreams. Although things are tight financially, I'm very appreciative and happy with my choice. So many times people stay in a career field they have no desire to be in because of fear. Instead of asking, "What if I fail" ask, "What if I succeed?" I speak from personal experience that the financial risk is not pretty, but choosing to stay simply for the consistent paychecks would've crippled my soul. Having the freedom to pursue my dreams and the ability to earn an uncapped amount of money is beautiful. Although having a consistent paycheck coming in brings comfort, bringing in an unlimited flow of income will bring wealth.

For the first time in my life I want something more than to be mother and wife, and as of this week I've realized for the first time that I really have plenty of time for that to become my reality. Coming from someone who's wanted to be a mother for 10+ years, that's a huge step.

The Joys of Retail

As the holidays approached it brought up another topic burning in my heart: the idea of Black Friday and the companies pulling millions of their associates away from their families year after year. Many stores have started to open earlier and earlier with most opening Thanksgiving Day. Although I'm disappointed in the companies for being inhumane, I'm mostly disappointed in consumers. If there weren't crowds of people waiting to rush into the stores, stores wouldn't feel the pressure to open earlier.

For that reason and more I vow to never participate in the Black Friday madness, especially when it falls on Thanksgiving Day. Retail employees are stretched thin during the holiday season, required to work excessive hours, and in most cases are seen as disposable almost immediately following the new year. This year it was rumored that in some areas Wal-Mart associates were protesting Black Friday. I'm not sure if they followed through but their jobs are at risk. In order for businesses to get it, consumers need to protest. The few bucks saved will make it worth it, right? How selfish! I promise you this, if customers don't show up, by the following year businesses would react.

Entrepreneurial Drive

Perseverance: steadfastness in doing something despite difficulty or delay in achieving success. Currently I find myself having to fight for the career I want, and I'm prepared to do just that. Although I may have the ability to do any and everything my heart wants, that doesn't mean it'll come easily. When it does come it'll make me appreciate things even more. I just have to realize that this is another test of my growth, patience, and faith in God.

As I sit here wide awake there is so much running through my mind. This is the 3rd time I am writing today, which is telling me there's a lot on my heart and mind. Yet I'm relatively at peace about it all. At this moment my mind is running with ideas of businesses and other entrepreneurial ventures I'd like to start. As I've gotten to know myself better I have realized that being an entrepreneur is the best fit for me. I'm very anxious to get started. I understand there is a process and that I have to work my way to the top, but I can finally see the bigger picture.

The funny part is the bigger the dream, the more I think about how I can help others, not only my family but also helping the community. I have full confidence that within the next 5-10 years I will be very successful. I will one day look back on the time of struggle and smile knowing that God has seen me through above and beyond my dreams. In the meantime I will continue to remain faithful in knowing that this is simply the calm before the storm.

Watching shows like Shark Tank fuel my internal desire to be successful as an entrepreneur. Although I do not have a particular product I'm looking to sell, the spirit of self-employment is motivating and encouraging for me. While life has been relatively slow, I've attempted to watch mostly shows that have some level of positive impact on my life and my future goals, dreams, and aspirations. In the meantime, I've been placing a large focus on developing myself professionally and financially. Things have been very tough financially, and I'm simply hoping they start to get better. Working two jobs has been draining but it's what I have to do to make up for my lost income.

Steadfastness

Lately, it seems that every moment of my day is filled with work. I'm simply hoping that it begins to pay off soon so that I can cut back the hours some. Maybe by the end of June I will be able to leave my part time job and actually enjoy life a bit more. At least that way I'll have my nights and weekends to myself to build my businesses, and more importantly build my future for the sake of my future children and I.

My biggest goal is to be able to buy a house by the end of the calendar year. That's the biggest desire of my heart at this point and I'm truly hoping I'm able to achieve this goal. It'll be the best birthday gift I could possibly give myself. In order to be able to do so, I must rebuild my credit and save some money, both of which seem like a significant struggle. Paying off credit cards would help, but living paycheck to paycheck makes it difficult to do so.

At this point it's completely in the hands of God! I don't know how but I'm trusting he will allow me the true desires of my heart! Until then I'm going to continue to do all that I can to reach my goals. Lately things have been extremely frustrating for me financially. I've been working extremely hard and financial results don't seem to be coming in fast enough. There's no worse feeling than working your butt off only to have your bank account in a negative state. At this point I'm doing everything I can think of to get back on my feet and figure out my next steps in life. Yesterday I did a good deal of reflecting, processing, and also planning. I reflected on the past year while also making goals for myself for this coming year.

Writing out some of the major events of the past year showed me that I made a lot of life decisions, all of which involved me leaving situations where I was unhappy. Whether it was moving down south, the break up with my ex, leaving my job, or deciding not to finish school, every major life decision made this past year was for me in my pursuit of happiness. The frustrating part of these reflections is that these areas in which I "cleaned house" have yet to be replaced. I'm trying to focus on the fact that I made space to be able to receive my blessings, but I have also spent this time figuring out what I truly want.

I feel that my goals for this coming year are very much attainable! The biggest goal being buying a home, I'm learning that it may not be happening this year, and learning to be okay if it doesn't happen. Knowing it will happen, just not on my timing, has been the biggest lesson for me to learn this past year. And who knows, maybe it will happen this year, but I won't allow the answer to that question to make or break me. Being able to plan out the next year brought me comfort that things will be okay. I have step-by-step plans of attack with check-points to keep me on track.

My mother expressed a concern about what may happen if I don't reach these goals. She feels that when I set goals for myself I tend to be very hard on myself. That's something I'm willing to consider working on, and evaluating my new goals are a great start! During this reflection time, I've set some very specific goals for myself for this year. Honestly I'm excited to accomplish every one of them. I know I can be hard on myself if I don't achieve my goals, but I plan to achieve them.

Mother and Wife

Lifelong Desire

I've wanted to be a mother for years at this point, and I've always convinced myself of why I shouldn't have children and instead I should wait. I think I've reached a place of why not? I have always firmly believed my childbearing years will expire at 30, but it is my hope to conceive a miracle of my own within the next year! Along with that I plan to get fully established in my new career, travel more often, buy a home, and pay off my debt. Wouldn't that make for such a great year? The icing on the cake of course would be to fall in love with someone I'm meant to be with. But unlike many other times in my life, romantic love will not be the primary life goal...just a really great bonus!

If you'd asked me where my life would be by 23, I would love to have been married with kids by now. In my grandmother's generation that was normal, perhaps even late, but in today's world I'm crazy for wanting that life so soon and I'm constantly encouraged to take my time. For years I've defined being a woman by her ability to be a great mother and wife. Growing up that is all that I aspired to do, and yet every time I express that desire I get told to wait!

Since when did wanting to be a mother become such a bad thing? There are girls becoming mothers as young as 13, but I'm crazy for wanting it at 23. Every time I log into social media, it's full of people getting married, engaged, or having babies. What's so wrong with wanting that for myself? It's almost as if people look at me as if I've evaded Ebola then I run around asking for it. Yes, I want other things in life, but a family is on top of the list. Sorry, not sorry!

Am I Really Ready?

Lately I've been thinking a lot about the want vs. need choice I've found myself making lately and I think I've answered my question. The debate itself shows me that I may not be ready for marriage and I was rushing myself out of fear that I'd somehow run out of time. I've created this timeline of life events for myself and the older I've gotten, the crazier it's made me knowing I'm not there. For me, being married no later than 24 and kids no later than 30 was the ultimate goal, but now I have adjusted my goals.

I've come to the realization that age 30 doesn't have to be the cut off for me to have kids. Maybe it doesn't have to take that long, but it won't be my main focus until I've reached these other goals I've set for myself. I want to finish grad school, travel the world, buy a home, buy a franchise, get married, and pay off my debts. If I happen to have a child before achieving my goals, obviously I will embrace and enjoy the experience, but I will not actively pursue that lifestyle until I have achieved the goals I have set for myself.

I think having these goals met will make me a stronger mother one day. As far as getting married, I'm going to enjoy my freedoms until I fall in love with someone who removes all doubts. When I fall in love with a person I want and need then I will commit the rest of my life to them. Throughout these past few months I've had a lot of growth and honestly I'm proud of that growth. I know I'm not even close to the person I want to be, but I'm far from the person I once was. Although I'm still in somewhat of a dark place, I know that within the next few months many of my sacrifices will be worth it.

Marriage shouldn't feel like a death sentence that you're waiting to end; it should be a commitment to be with one person by choice. I saw a quote saying "Marriage is like deleting all songs on your iPod but 1." Really, if you think about it...it's true. You're choosing one person to spend the rest of your life with...why not choose your favorite option? Until the guy I want is also the guy I need, I'm going to enjoy life as much as possible.

This year I'm truly committing to putting myself first. I think this is the first time in my adult life I will be making decisions for me and me alone. Shortly after graduating college, I ended up in a serious relationship with my now ex-boyfriend. Almost immediately, every decision I made factored him in. Obviously this is the respectful thing to do when in a relationship, but what I didn't realize was that along the way I was losing myself. It wasn't until after the breakup that I realized I had no idea who I was as an adult and as an individual. Every part of my identity, desires, and goals were in some way connected to him.

I think having that realization has allowed me clarity in my life in order to find my own dreams. For the longest I felt my identity was solely through being a mother and wife. Consequently, not being married or pregnant made me feel invaluable as a woman. For so long that was all I could see being my true purpose in life; it was all that I truly wanted, but now, I'm very thankful that I didn't accidentally conceive a baby or rush into a doomed marriage. I'm finally realizing that once I experience a happier and healthier life for myself, I will be ready to experience that part of life.

They say if you want to hear God laugh, just tell him your plans. Well for me my plan was to be engaged by the time I graduated college, married by 21, and kids by 25. So from that perspective, I am very behind schedule. But from my new perspective I am nowhere near ready for any of that because I haven't had the chance to experience life and get to know me yet.

I once heard Beyonce say that she didn't' feel she should get married before age 25 because she didn't truly know herself yet. Well, now I understand where she's coming from. And although she's often criticized for having overly sexual lyrics and dances, with regards to her personal life she got it right. She married her best friend, maintained her virginity until marriage, enjoyed her marriage for a few years, and then had a child...all while progressing forward in a successful career. Although I can't quite sing like her (supposedly), I really think a lot can be learned from her on both a personal and professional level. Maybe one day our paths will cross and I will get to tell her. Until then I'm focusing on me.

Paradigm Shift

Now that I have learned to find my value and worth it's completely different. Although I would love to be a mother and wife, that's no longer my only goal in life. I now know there are so many goals for me to accomplish in addition to being a mother and wife. After our break up, my ex asked me what were my goals in life and the only goals I'd had were to be a mother and wife. He then asked what goals do I have that don't involve another person. I can now list quite a few goals solely dependent on my efforts. So until those family goals happen naturally, I am focused on making my other goals happen.

The biggest problem with my worth being associated solely with being a wife and mother is that it makes me feel worthless, and the longer I'm single, the further I am from having value. Well, thankfully, I have learned to find my value outside of being a wife and mother. School has been a source of frustration, particularly this semester. I cannot WAIT to be done with school because it's truly irritating! I often times wonder why I decided to pursue graduate school and if I'll ever use the degree, but it's too late now. For me school has never been much of a choice, particularly undergrad. I went to college because society practically demands it, but all in all I would much rather have received my MRS degree than an MBA or even PhD.

One thing that has not been made clear to me is that my hopes of getting married young...just won't be. I find myself wanting children so badly, but, as I was reminded yesterday, I need to be in a stable relationship first. I created a boundaries chart for my dating and friend relationships. These boundaries will help me to manage my expectations appropriately and also classify people in my life effectively. My hope is that being able to reference and apply these boundaries will protect my heart. Maybe one day I will have the relationship I desire, the family I want, and lifelong friendships I feel I deserve. Until then I will continue to improve myself in preparation. "Everything you're going through now is preparing you for what you want."

Lately I've been extremely busy and putting more and more on my plate. For me being busy is a good thing! Having a lot to keep me preoccupied serves as a distraction from my chronic baby fever. I have so many things that I want to accomplish in life to prepare for a happy and healthy family. One thing I'm learning to realize is that growth, development, and accomplishments are the pre-work to be ready for my dreams. Ensuring that I'm emotionally and financially stable prior to getting married and especially before kids will prove to be beneficial. Having my affairs in order prior to having kids will contribute to having a healthy and happy family, not just a family likely to be dysfunctional.

Waiting to have kids may be difficult for me, but it'll be worth it! I've seen plenty of cases where people have children accidentally and end up struggling to make ends meet. Then there are cases where a couple has waited until they were ready to start a family and they're in a much better place. This includes emotionally, financially, professionally, mentally (meaning their marriage is healthier), and just all around in a better place. I've recently come to the realization that I'm far from ready for kids. Before feeling ready, I need to grow emotionally, become financially stable, and professionally established. Additionally, I would like to be married first. I think being in a healthy marriage prior to having kids will give my children the comfort of a healthy family unit! Recently I adopted a dog, which has taught me I have very little patience, especially as needed to be ready for children. Maybe having full responsibility for a dog will teach me patience, but currently that's an area of opportunity for me!

Mother's Day was the day I thought my dreams would be coming true, the day I thought my ex and I would be getting married. Instead of getting married, I laid in my bed alone with zero possibility of getting married any time soon.

Prior to breaking up with my ex, my only true dream, goal, or aspiration was to be a mother and wife. To walk away from someone willing to give me that was one of the hardest things I could've ever done. Although I have zero desire to rekindle things with him, the looming date left things very heavy on my heart. I even wrote him an email expressing how I feel and he pretty much blew me off, but that's okay because it was helpful for me to get it off my chest.

Lately I've been taking a very passive approach to dating with the understanding that God will bring the right person into my life. At times that gets extremely lonely! In the meantime I'm focusing on being a better me emotionally, physically, and professionally. I'm so beyond thankful that my mother is who she is in my life. We may not always see eye to eye, but she's my rock and I appreciate her for that.

I truly hope one day I can be a great mother like her! Not any time soon, but when it's meant to happen. The sacrifice, unconditional love, discipline, and care she's given is truly invaluable in my life! Ironically enough, I've finally reached a place where I can genuinely say I'm not ready to be a mother. As much as I would love to have a family, I'm not in a position to be a wife or a mother. There are things I need to accomplish in order to be ready for that life! I'm taking some time to be selfish and focus on my goals, so that when I do have a family I'm ready to be selfless. I need to establish myself both professionally and financially, along with developing emotionally, in order to be ready to be the mother and wife I dream of being. I keep telling myself...in due time.

What does Marriage Look Like?

I read an article on Facebook about the ways people who were raised by a single parent love differently. Ultimately, I found it very accurate. It discussed how we are hesitant to trust, but when we do it's whole-heartedly. The fear of abandonment is strong, and we're naturally skeptical to believe in the happily ever after fairytale. That last part struck the closest to home for me because lasting love feels like a unicorn that I'm determined exists. I didn't have exposure to successful marriages. So for me to have a burning desire to have a successful marriage seems silly.

To me, a successful marriage is no more defined by length of time together than age defines being a responsible adult. Having a successful marriage involves being in love with the person you're committed to for the rest of your life. In my opinion this excludes people who stay together for the kids or because it's just easer to stay married. It is my deepest desire to be madly in love with my husband for decades to come after we say I do. But then the question becomes how? What does that even look like, and is that even possible? Who do I turn to for marital advice, when there aren't any successful marriages around me?

Disclaimer: this is my definition of a successful marriage. There may be other versions of marriages in my life, but I feel that getting advice should come from a person I aspire to be like, at least in that area. For some, a successful marriage is defined as never getting divorced. But for me, that's not good enough. I know one day I will get to experience a true and lasting love that I'm trusting in God for. Until then I will continue to develop myself into the person who is ready, able, and worthy of lasting love. God will bless me for wanting to honor his will.

Being single sucks at times, especially when your biggest desire is to be apart of a family. After working two jobs, all I want is to come home to someone who loves me and plans to stay around. I refuse to believe that it's within God's will for me to be lonely and I'm doing everything within my power to prepare for my blessing. At the end of the day true companionship, intimacy, and love are critical parts of life. Truthfully, these are parts of life that I feel that I deserve.

I am asking God and believing that he will bring my husband into my life and make it abundantly clear that he is the right one for me. I feel that I am ready to meet my husband and have grown enough to handle the relationship in a healthy and mature manner. I deserve to be with someone long term in a happy and healthy committed relationship. I deserve someone who wants to build towards marriage and a family. Someone who is a good fit for me, who challenges me to be better, and is naturally compatible with me. Most importantly, I deserve someone who is going to walk into my life and never walk out of it.

It is my prayer that God reveals my husband to me. I want to be with someone who brings comfort, stability, and consistency to my life. Ironically all of the opposites I experienced with my relationship with my father. It's amazing how much a bad relationship can teach you if you pay attention to the lessons. Leaving the doors to my past closed has not been an easy task by any means, but I have seen it has been a very healthy decision so far. How can I expect to truly move on if I continue to revisit the past? The answer is that I can't or it will be a very unproductive method.

I hope to meet someone with genuine intentions, a desire to build a healthy relationship, and is just as tired of the games as I am. Not only do I hope it, but I believe it will happen. God built us to be relational creatures and he honors the union of marriage. If my desire is in line with his will, why wouldn't he allow it? I keep telling myself when the time is right I'll meet him, but it's really getting harder and harder to remain patient. At this point, even if not my husband, I am asking for a serious committed relationship and that is what I'm ready for at this point in my life.

There are times that I wish being single didn't hurt so bad, and most of the time being busy during the day I don't realize it, but at night it hits me pretty hard. Wanting that special person to share life with but not having them is a hard pill to swallow. I have to sometimes catch myself and not allow the lack of a relationship to diminish my self-worth or lower my standards; doing so will only lead to problems. I've made entirely too much progress to build my self-esteem to allow one lonely thought to kill it completely. It's not fair to me nor is it fair to the person I grew from.

Black Lives Matter

One issue that has been deep on my heart is the racism and hatred filling this country. Over the past year or so there has been a lot of hate, racist conversations, murders, police brutality, and protests. I feel it must be similar to how it felt during the Civil Rights era and honestly it makes me extremely uncomfortable. Today for the first time I genuinely feared getting pulled over. Not feared getting a ticket, but feared a ticket would be the least of my worries. I think it's a sad day in America when those whose mission is to protect and serve are the most feared group of people. This is in large part due to extreme cases of abuse of power and those officers being protected and defended.

At this time, more than anything, race is constantly a part of the conversation...and in most cases unnecessarily so. There are people of all races judging a person's character based on the color of his or her skin and it's despicable. Making racial generalizations based on the actions of a particular person is racist. Racism is a learned hatred or fear for someone based on the color of that person's skin. When I have children I will do my best to raise my children as color-blind as possible. It's my prayer that by minimizing racial conversations, my children will love and accept people regardless of their race.

Not just a person's race, but I also want my children to love and accept people regardless of gender, sexual orientation, religion, occupation, or anything. I feel this world is too judgmental and too quick to label someone. My dream is to live in a world where labels don't matter, but my fear is that won't happen. However, to the best of my ability I will create a world for my future children and teach them to love the heart, character, and mind of another. I swear this country is continuing to get worse and worse. I may seriously consider moving to another country within the next 5-10 years. I don't know how I'm supposed to want to live here; it is so far from the best country in the world. I just don't see this country being a good place to raise my future children.

As I've gotten older, I've learned to appreciate and aspire to the idea of black love. Not only in a romantic manner, but also loving my race as a whole. To me this means supporting, embracing, and encouraging the members of the black community. One concept I wish was more commonly accepted is that pro-black does not mean anti-white. You can love your race without having negative feelings towards people of other races. Preferences do not excuse prejudices. This frustrates me to the extent that sometimes I seriously consider living in a different country. I just do not like where things are going in this country. We are no longer living in the best country in the world, and it's considered blasphemy to say otherwise, but if you take an unbiased look at this country you will see...we're far from the best country.

Lately I've been getting more and more frustrated with the racial injustice in our country. Police brutality has been increasingly excessive, particularly against the black community. Between the shootings, hanging, killings, strangling, etc., it's truly getting out of hand. The day before my birthday there will be a million man march in DC and I fully plan to attend. If you remain silent during times of oppression you are choosing the side of the oppressor. With that being said, my days of remaining silent while my people are being killed off are no longer an option. The black community has been taken from their homeland, enslaved, separated from their family, treated as personal property, raped, whipped, discriminated against, belittled, and hated. Any time any of those things are referenced we're encouraged to pretend it all is in the past. America loves black culture but hates black people. Enough is enough!

"If you stick a knife in my back 9 inches and you pull it out 6 inches, that's not progress. If you pull it all the way out that's not progress. The progress comes from healing the wound that the blow made. They haven't begun to pull the knife out...they won't even admit the knife is there." –Malcolm X. We as a black community need to rally together and uplift ourselves. Clearly this country is not going to help support us. We have to do that for ourselves. Personally, I'm ready, willing, and able to do my part to better my black community.

A large part of why I want to own several different businesses is to embrace and develop leaders within the black community. I want to support black businesses and professionals. For my goods and services, I will choose to buy black. It is burning within my soul to create a business that serves, uplifts, and betters my people. That is how I plan to do my part. There's a lot of work to be done in order to heal our wounds, but day-by-day we can make efforts towards change. I'm praying for my people! We need healing and true progression as we are living in a country that doesn't love us. They see us as entertainment, devalue our lives, and they see this as the norm.

Final Thoughts

This past year was nothing at all as I expected, but it was a necessary year of growth. The deeper I got into the problems I'd been facing, the more sub-problems I found along the way. There were several points where I questioned what wasn't wrong with me. Despite it all, I pushed through and took life one day at a time. As much turmoil as I went through, I know that means the blessings are around the corner. They have to be, I believe in that 100%. There's no other logical purpose other than to prepare me for the good that's coming. I've been pushed, tested, and frustrated...and yet still I rise. I certainly rose to the occasion.

Through the changes in my career and professional journey, I've learned to trust God through it all. He has shown me that if I do my best He'll make a way to cover me through the rest. There were several months where I literally had no clue how my bills were going to be paid. I still have a place to live, my car, and food to eat, even during the five months where I had no income at all. With this process/challenge I've learned a lot and grown strength in character. I've learned to trust God more that I ever have and my ability to pray through the good and bad has heightened to a place I didn't realize was possible for me!

Throughout this development I have also become an independent Christian, meaning I'm developing a personal relationship with God on my own. In the past, my attendance to church was highly motivated by who was going with me. Now my relationship has 100% to do with me and is growing every day. I've learned to tithe faithfully and trust that God is allowing me to sow into my financial stability. I began having daily bible study in the mornings to start my day focused on my spiritual development. That, to me, is the most growth I've even experienced and that I'm the most proud of to say the least.

My friendships have been a continued struggle for me, but I think things have gotten better along the way. I have learned to manage and uphold healthy expectations, but most importantly, I've learned how to effectively communicate my needs and make less emotional decisions. This has allowed me to say to someone "Hey when you did _____ it made me feel like _____ because _____." Where as before I would bottle things in and assume the other person would know I was upset and I'd expect them to probe.

Understanding this balance has proven to be beneficial to my friendships but also my romantic encounters. It has also given me a chance to make logical decisions and communicate in an effective manner. I tell people what I need or what has disappointed me and give them a chance to response. They'll either take steps to fix or change the issue, or will choose not to care. From there I can make a healthy decision based on my needs.

Dating has been very much a whirlwind over the last year, but my faith stands strong. Not only do I believe that I will find the right guy for me, but I also believe this is my preparation for The One too. The challenges, struggles, and lessons learned are preparing me for my future husband. Although marriage is very much a goal of mine, I'd rather wait until I'm ready (and he's ready), knowing the marriage will last a lifetime. For me, divorce is not an option so I'll wait to make sure he's the man I'm supposed to be with. In the meantime, I'm learning to be a better version of myself and ensuring I'm deserving of a healthy family and marriage. Being able to develop my weaker relationship skills is necessary to get to the marriage I want.

The funny part is how my ex used to tell me all the time how "we" weren't ready for marriage. I would always respond how I was ready and he wasn't. Looking back I really wasn't...honestly I still may not be, but now I'm working towards being ready. When the time is right things will happen naturally, and it will very much be worth the wait when that moment comes.

Being an adult gets really hard sometimes, but it will prove to be worth it all. For starters having to pay bills is the biggest frustration of being an adult, but I know it requires responsibility to have the things I want in life. A few things I want to develop consistency around include traveling more often, a consistent workout plan, and taking the time for the things I want in life. I would love for this year to be a year of financial growth and stability. I continuously pray for healing and development.

I would also like this year to be a year of healthy relationships (romantic and otherwise). Of these things I'm praying and believing God to bring them into my life.

Living on my own has been such a beautiful thing. I used to get lonely living alone, but now I very much appreciate it. Being able to have my own space and create a safe haven in my home brings me great peace. My biggest desire is to grow in life towards my goals of being an entrepreneur. That is my top priority at this point. Organizing myself professionally is what my biggest focus is on currently. I feel that once I get myself in order professionally and financially everything else will fall into place.

Only time will tell!

Connect with the Author

Website: www.nicolesnetwork.com

Email: tiara.nicolesnetwork@gmail.com

Facebook: Nicole's Network

YouTube: Nicole's Network

Instagram: @TiaraNicole1011

Twitter: @TiaraNicole1011

Made in the USA
Middletown, DE
23 January 2018